The Best of Joe Weider's

MUSCLE
& FITNESS

Women's Weight Training and Bodybuilding Tips and Routines

The Best of Joe Weider's

MUSCLE & FITNESS

Women's Weight Training and Bodybuilding Tips and Routines

Contemporary Books, Inc.
Chicago

Library of Congress Cataloging in Publication Data

Women's weight training and bodybuilding tips and routines.

    1. Bodybuilding—for women—Addresses, essays, lectures.   2. Physical fitness for women—Addresses, essays, lectures.   I. Weider, Betty.   II. Weider, Joe.   III. Muscle & Fitness
GV546.6.W64B47   1982   646.7'5   81-69616
ISBN 0-8092-5755-6   AACR2
ISBN 0-8092-5754-8 (pbk.)

All photos courtesy of IFBB

Published by Contemporary Books, Inc.
180 North Michigan Avenue, Chicago, Illinois 60601
Manufactured in the United States of America
Library of Congress Catalog Card Number: 81-69616
International Standard Book Number: 0-8092-5755-6 (cloth)
                                  0-8092-5754-8 (paper)

Published simultaneously in Canada by
Beaverbooks, Ltd.
150 Lesmill Road
Don Mills, Ontario M3B 2T5
Canada

Contents

Exercise Fact, Fantasy, and Enchantment

by Sue Meyerott

Becky, a sedentary, overweight, 35-year-old woman, came into the spa as she had every day now for a week, to get rid of her overabundance of fat. Becky was never one to enjoy exercising so this spa was ideal for her. Her daily routine at the spa consisted of a five-minute set of spot reducing exercises to remove fat from her hips and thighs; a 30-minute workout on the roller machine that massages the hips and thighs to break the fat up in these problem areas while the individual relaxes; and a half-hour in the sauna to melt the fat off. Every day Becky left the spa feeling accomplished because after her "workout" the scale at the spa showed she had lost two pounds. However, the next day she seemed to gain back those two pounds. "I wonder," she thought, "I've heard that exercise increases your appetite . . . I must be eating more."

Becky, like many people, seeks the magic pill: a weight control program with little or no work. Today there are so many fads that sell promises of something for nothing that by now you may find yourself confused. What is fact and what is fantasy? What CAN various types of exercise do for you? How can you tell exercise fact from

Sue Meyerott instructs obesity-control and physical conditioning classes at UCLA.

fantasy without losing the enchantment of exercise? Let's examine a few of the major exercise myths that Becky and others believe.

1

EXERCISE FACT AND FANTASY

MYTH: Exercise is bad for weight control because it builds up muscles. You will gain weight, not lose it.

FACT: Each type of exercise is specific in the effects it will produce. Some exercises will "tone up" or strengthen your muscles without improving your cardiovascular system or removing fat. Exercises that call for high resistance/low repetitions, such as lifting 100 pounds one time only, will have the greatest tendency to build muscles. Women, however, because of a difference in sex hormones, do not have the same capacity to develop bulging muscles as male bodybuilders. Weight lifting exercises that call for low resistance/high repetitions, such as lifting 10 pounds 20 times, will tone muscles without making them bulge in men or women. Thus by choosing the proper type of strength training exercises, you don't have to worry about "overdeveloped" muscles.

Endurance-type exercises—walking, jogging, swimming and bicycling—fall into the category of low resistance/high repetition exercises and therefore will not develop protruding muscles, only shapely ones.

Will exercise make you weigh more? Muscle tissue is denser than fat tissue. Exercise of any type will encourage your body to hold on to more of its muscle tissue than if you were sedentary. Even if you don't lose weight, you will look and feel slimmer because your body will become more dense, more compact. That is, when you add muscle tissue by exercising, you lose fat tissue. Basically, more of the calories you consume go into making muscle and less calories go into making fat. It is the quality of the weight on your body that is important, not the quantity. If you could weigh 150 pounds and look like you weighed 110 pounds at 5'5", weight wouldn't matter.

MYTH: If you want to lose fat from your "problem areas," spot reducing is the best method.

FACT: The concept of spot reducing for reduction of fat in a problem area, such as in the thighs or hips, is not supported by scientific evidence. It appears that we are all born with or develop at an early age a given number of fat cells. Once we have a fat cell we can't get rid of it. We can only reduce it in size. Not only do we have a certain number of fat cells in our bodies, but it appears we have a certain number of fat cells in specific areas of our bodies. Thus when we exercise a specific area, we can only reduce

the size of the fat cells not the number.

The question you must ask is: how effective is spot reducing for burning up fat? The answer is, not very effective. Spot reducing is just another name for calisthenics, which is a form of weight training without weights. Spot reducing is a misleading term since it implies that you can burn up fat with this method, which is incorrect. Weight training, calisthenics and spot reducing are all forms of strength training that may burn a

The superbly conditioned Rachel McLish, Ms. Olympia.

high number of calories per minute, but most people won't do them long enough for the number of calories to be a significant factor. In addition, scientific evidence suggests that the most effective type of exercise for specifically burning up fat is one that is an endurance exercise, such as walking, running, swimming or bicycling.

Does this mean that calisthenics and weight training are ineffective exercises? *NO!* It just means that for burning fat, they are not the most effective exercises. They do, however, play a very important function for anyone interested in having an attractive body (all of us). They are important for helping us shape our muscles in specific areas. In summary, spot reducing may not be effective in reducing fat in a certain area, but it can be effective in toning up the muscles and improving flexibility of the joints.

MYTH: An exercise is effective in weight control only if it is performed at the highest intensity possible to burn up the most calories.

FACT: The ideal exercise for fat control is an endurance exercise of low to moderate intensity and long duration. To burn up the most amount of fat the exercise should not be of high intensity. Why is this? At higher levels of exercise, fat is prohibited from being released from the fat cells so your body is unable to use it as a source of energy. In addition, if there is less fat available for fuel, your body will use up its sugar stores more readily. When your body's sugar stores get below a minimal level, you will experience fatigue and have to stop exercising. Studies show that the longer you exercise, the more fat you will burn for energy.

For example, in the first minute of exercise you may be burning 10 calories per minute, but less than one of those calories is derived from fat.

After one hour of exercise, you may be burning 10 calories per minute and nine of those calories are derived from fat. To exercise for an extended period of time, you can't exercise at a high intensity. In addition, each type of exercise is very specific in the effects it will produce. What you are trying to do is *train* your body to encourage the most amount of calories to be burned up, and more specifically, the *most amount of fat to be burned.*

When you choose an endurance type of activity which is rhythmic in nature, of low to moderate intensity and is done for an extended period of time (15–16 minutes), you are training your body to adapt to that exercise. The benefits are fantastic. Your muscles will learn to preferentially use fat, you will not fatigue as rapidly as you did when you were sedentary, and therefore you will burn more calories and fat. These are *not* the same benefits you would receive if you were to choose an exercise such as sprinting which is a high intensity/low duration exercise. *Training effects are very specific.*

MYTH: Walking isn't exercise.

FACT: Oh, how *wrong!* Walking is an exercise in which almost everyone may participate, and it is one of the best for weight control. Obese individuals have been found to walk only half the distance daily that lean individuals do, that is they seem to "save" steps. Walking can be done between activities, at all times of the day and anywhere. It is an endurance activity of low to moderate intensity and can be done daily for an extended period of time without a person straining muscles.

For a sedentary individual starting an exercise habit for weight control, walking is ideal. Becky would have burned up at least 300 calories in the hour she spent at the spa if she had walked during that time. In one week, that would add up to 2100 calories burned up by walking one hour per day for exercise. In addition, Becky,

who was sedentary, would begin to derive a training effect which would encourage more fat to be burned up. To continue improving she would have to walk a little faster and eventually want to jog, but that would be a natural progression. As your body adapts to exercise through frequent training sessions, the same level of exercise that exhausted you when you started your exercise habit will become a breeze. No longer will you breathe heavily or have your heart pound while walking at your normal pace. You will naturally begin to walk faster. *Exercise does not have to hurt to be effective.*

A good rule to follow with walking is to walk at a fast pace, slightly faster than your "normal" pace. In terms of calories, you will burn up the same number of calories walking a given distance as you would if you ran the distance. Why would a person want to jog then? The effects of exercise are not only in effect during the exercise session. They stay with you throughout the day as you get a training effect. An individual who is more fit in terms of endurance activities will *burn more fat at rest than the less fit individual.*

MYTH: Passive spot reducing machines are great for massaging the fat away.

FACT: The statement above would be true if a few words were left out: Passive spot reducing machines are great for massaging . . . *period!* As stated earlier, exercising a specific area—so-called spot reducing—is not an effective method for reducing fat in that area. Furthermore, if you use a machine that shakes or rolls you, as Becky did, calories may be burned up—by the machine, *not you!* These machines are ideal for relaxing your muscle, but not for burning fat or calories. A workout on these machines is *not exercise.*

MYTH: Sitting in a sauna is great for burning up calories.

FACT: Again, by deleting a few words, we can make the statement above true: Sitting in a sauna is great (if you enjoy it). You cannot cook your fat away! The assumption is, if you sweat or feel uncomfortable, you must be burning calories. Like Becky, you may lose weight by sitting in the sauna for a half hour, but the weight you lose will be water weight. You are dehydrating your body and will gain the weight back when you inevitably consume fluids.

MYTH: Exercise will automatically increase my appetite.

FACT: The relationship between exercise and appetite is not that clear-cut. There is, however, a very interesting inverse relationship of which sedentary individuals should take note. In many animal studies, it was found that if an animal's physical activity was restricted below a minimal level of exercise, the animal *increased* its food intake, not decreased. It has also been demonstrated in animal studies that exercise of low to moderate intensity did not increase the animal's appetite. The evidence indicates that a sedentary individual could only benefit from a moderate increase in exercise. In Becky's case, her exercise program was *not* exercise. Her daily weight fluctuation of two pounds was due to variations of water levels—not due to any effect exercise may have had on appetite. Becky did not have the facts about exercise and came to a seemingly reasonable but incorrect conclusion.

CAPTURING THE ENCHANTMENT OF EXERCISE

It is only through acquiring the facts about exercise that you will be able to choose an exercise plan wisely. If you rely on myths, you will not understand why you have been unsuccessful in attaining your goals. If you, like Becky, are seeking the magic pill for weight control, exercise is the answer. All exercises are ideal for something. You must determine whether the exercises you are participating in or are about to begin are right for you. To make an exercise work for you, you must make the exercise enjoyable.

How do you capture the enchantment of exercise? Exercise charm lies in the magic that makes fat disappear, the illusion of weighing less as you change your body composition and that extraordinary good feeling after exercising. Exercise can also have a spell-binding effect on you, if it specifically suits your needs.

If you are just starting an exercise habit you will want to slowly add exercise into your daily routine. To help exercise retain its power over you, it must be something that you enjoy doing.

There are several ways to decide which exercises are best for you. The first path is to choose an exercise according to the benefits your body will derive from it. Endurance activities such as walking, cross-country skiing, and roller skating are best for burning up fat, while calisthenics and weight training exercises are best for shaping up muscles in specific areas. Your ideal exercise plan would include exercises to improve flexibility (stretches) and cardiovascular fitness, control fat (endurance exercises) and strengthen and tone specific muscle groups (weight training exercises). But, most of us are not ideal humans. We are hesitant to jump into a total exercise program just because we know it is good for us. How, then, can we increase the likelihood that we will start an exercise habit and keep it?

To increase the probability that you will start and maintain your exercise habit, pick an exercise that fits your personality and movement style. Each of us has a different personality type and body type which lends itself to different preferences for body movement. Some individuals feel most comfortable doing sustained, low intensity activities that are free flowing, such as walking or jogging. Some people enjoy high energy, static activities such as weight lifting. To begin your exercise habit, choose an exercise that best fits your movement style, then add the other types of exercise into your repertoire.

Remember, *it's your choice*. Exercise is something you do for yourself. It is something to be enjoyed. To capture the enchantment of exercise, you must find the power its charm holds specifically for you!

Aerobic exercise, such as running, helps to control obesity.

Is Strength a Matter of Sex?

by Julie Ann Butler

Remember the days when men were men and women were glad of it? Boys wore blue, girls wore pink and haircuts told the difference. Girls played house, while boys played sports and the exceptions were ostracized to be tomboys and sissies. Women were the weaker sex.

Today, the individual takes precedence over male or female. Haircuts are unisex, men are allowed to cry and women are discovering their physical selves. Myths about the inferiority of women are being questioned along with societal norms and differences in strength are diminishing. Men are still stronger than women, but now physiologists are debating why.

Five years ago, men were assumed to be biologically superior. Men were taller, leaner, they weighed more, had bigger hearts and lungs and a higher hemoglobin content.

Athletic training for women was feared to increase their growth rate, create bulky muscles, and a less-feminine appearance. "Exercises must be properly designed to improve femininity," one book warned. A female seldom sweated doing knee-bent push-ups, playing six-man basketball and choosing not to participate during her menstrual cycle. Research confirmed the inferiority complex.

The average college-age female is fatter (25 vs. 15% fat), lighter (average difference of 40 pounds) and has a lower lean body weight (average difference of 46 pounds) when compared to the average college male. In 1975, Herbert De Vries reported that women are twice as susceptible to injury as men, especially in events like sprinting and jumping where the female's musculoskeletal system was at a disadvantage.

Women were reportedly less responsive to training than their male counterparts and they showed only half as much improvement in motor skills as men. Because of their inferior aerobic capacity, they were discouraged from running over 1000 meters.

Today, women are running marathons and physiologists are saying that the male hormone testosterone *might* be the reason men test stronger than women. That biochemical factors like genetics and body composition are more accurate determinants of strength and athletic prowess. And that sociological and psychological factors play an immeasurable part in deciding one's strength.

A study of world records reveals that where both men's and women's records exist, the

5

female's athletic performance is usually 10% or more below the male's. But the comparison is misleading. The best female 400-meter freestyle swimmer in 1970 was swimming faster in her event than the best male in the mid-1950s.

The progress is encouraging, especially in light of the fact that the female's training program and coaching have been lacking. Remember in 1976, when U.S. Olympian swimmer Shirley Babashoff lost five medals to the East German women because she refused to lift weights? "I don't want to develop muscles like a man," she alibied. America understood and some accused the East German girls of taking anabolic steroids.

For the record, women are typically weaker than men when tested for absolute strength. And steroids will have little if any effect on a woman's physique because women lack the androgen receptors necessary for protein synthesis and muscle hypertrophy.

Differences are glaring in tests of upper body strength, where the female is 43–63% weaker, in contrast to lower body strength, where the female is only 27% weaker. This is because

women walk, ride bikes and climb stairs to develop lower body strength, while they seldom lift heavy boxes and until recently open their own doors.

If strength is expressed relative to body weight, the difference is reduced to 7%, and the female is actually 5.8% stronger when strength is expressed relative to lean body weight.

Several studies have shown that women athletes on weight training programs can substantially increase their strength with little muscular hypertrophy. The strength of a trained female was considerably higher than untrained males of similar age, but well below the strength of male weight lifters.

Muscle hypertrophy is related to the plasma production rate of testosterone, thus men will gain muscle bulk to a greater extent than women. Certain females with naturally high endogenous levels of testosterone will tend to bulk similar to males, thus explaining the physiques of the East German women.

These strength differences between males and females are not apparent until puberty (age 12–15), at which time there is a rapid rise in the strength of the male's muscles and a leveling off of the female's strength. Most physiologists agree that the hormones testosterone and estrogen are the cause, but recent studies blame societal conditioning and genetics as well.

Both men and women secrete testosterone, but men secrete 5–10 mg/day versus 0.1 mg/day for women. Testosterone has been given to laboratory animals and sedentary men yielding results such as aggressive behavior, bone density, lean body mass, muscle glycogen storage and muscle protein synthesis.

Aggressive behavior is determined by too many cultural and psychological factors to be linked solely to testosterone. But testosterone may be the cause of a thicker bone, because it stimulates both the production of the protein matrix and the retention of calcium by bones.

There is no solid evidence that testosterone is responsible for increases in lean body mass and body mass in response to weight training and other types of vigorous exercise. Bodybuilders report large weight increases as a result of weight training and steroids, but the training program and diet are not to be discounted. The results might also be due to a placebo effect.

Muscle glycogen stores in castrated laboratory animals can be increased by injections of testosterone. Since glycogen levels in skeletal muscle also rise within two days after exhaustive exercise, some physiologists think that testosterone aids in glycogen supercompensation.

Testosterone has a stimulating effect on amino acid uptake, RNA synthesis and DNA synthesis, resulting in muscle protein synthesis and a greater chance for muscle hypertrophy (growth). Men have more androgen receptors than women, although this is genetically determined. Men also have a greater range of both slow-twitch and fast-twitch muscle fibers (80–90% range versus a 40–60% range for women). Fast-twitch fibers in men hypertrophy upon weightlifting.

In contrast, the female hormone estrogen increases body fat and has a slight atrophying effect on muscles. It allows less protein synthesis and inhibits sweating (a plus for women swimmers, creating better buoyancy and insulation). It also limits cholesterol in the arteries, lessening the chance of coronary heart disease in women.

The assumption that men are biologically superior to women is made without regard to sociological factors like experience and training. A test of motor fitness showed that boys and girls are equal until puberty, which explains why girls can compete with boys in little league baseball. After puberty, men throw the softball farther than women with their dominant arm, but tests with the non-dominant arm show men and women to be equal. The difference is training, and, until recently, women have been afforded very little.

A good example of this is found in long distance running. Women used to run no more than 1000 meters. Today they are running marathons and using overtraining methods similar to men. Women runners have relative body fats well below those of the average college-age female and many are below the average for the college-age male. The average woman has a 22–24% lean–fat ratio versus 15% for men. Female distance runners are generally lean, like their male counterparts. Here, body composition is paramount to sex. World-class distance runner Julie Brown has 7% relative body fat, comparable to the best men marathoners (5%).

Therefore, one's maximal aerobic capacity (necessary for endurance) is often genetic and more often influenced by factors other than sex. In general, men have a 50% advantage, but expressed in terms of body weight, the difference is reduced to 20%. If one's aerobic capacity is expressed relative to lean body mass, the discrepancy is 7%. Like tests of strength, women who train harder will exceed the capacity of untrained men. Since women have smaller hearts, lungs and a lower hemoglobin content, they work closer to their maximum aerobic capacity during submaximal tasks like a marathon race.

In 1975, women were encouraged to run distance as opposed to sprints to avoid utilizing fast-twitch muscle fibers which were supposedly weaker in women. The advice would be detrimental to women with a predominance of fast-twitch muscle fibers. Again, one's fitness is a bigger factor in aerobic capacity than sex.

Another myth was that women should not exercise during menstruation or pregnancy. In the Tokyo Olympics, 41% of 66 women questioned reported a disturbance in menstrual flow. Performance was altered in 17%, but results were both positive and negative, thus inconclusive.

In the old days, athletic women were thought to develop tense, unyielding abdominal walls that hinder normal delivery. Although women are unable to perform at top level during pregnancy, moderate exercise strengthens muscles leading to an easier labor—87.2% shorter labor and less complications (50% fewer Caesarian sections). The pregnancy usually means improved future performances.

In 1973, Jack Wilmore described the female athlete as significantly taller, with a higher functional capacity, greater heart volume, total hemoglobin and vital capacity than the average female. He forgot to mention the nonbiological thicker skin she needed to ignore societal norms and continue to train.

Today, that pressure is gone and the myths about big muscles and masculinity are dispelled. The opportunity for all women to become physically fit has never been better. The stronger individual overshadows stereotypes of the weaker sex. Today, women are women and men are glad of it.

Kathy Bassacker (left) and Ellen Davis are both successful competitive bodybuilders, and both women quickly regained their winning form after giving birth.

How to Start and Maintain an Exercise Habit

by Sue Meyerott

You've done it again. You can't stand yourself or your body any longer. Last night you stuffed that last piece of candy in your already bursting stomach, knowing you really didn't want it. You look at yourself in the mirror with disgust. Playing with your fat rolls, you turn away and resolve, "THIS TIME for sure! I'm going on a diet and exercise program if it kills me."

The first day you exercise you feel great. Some of the guilty feelings subside as you plunge into your exercise program with a beginner's enthusiasm. "Nothing will stop me THIS TIME," you pledge sincerely. For two weeks straight you don't miss one day of exercise. You are sure THIS TIME it will be different. Then it happens, just as you knew it would: the exercise program is terminated.

The first day you fail to exercise you swear it is only for today, while in the back of your mind you can feel the guilt begin. The magic has been broken; you now fear the lack of self-control. Rather than face the guilt of failure you say "oh-what-the hell" and plunge back into your "normal" sedentary lifestyle.

How many times have you started an exercise program just to abandon it, feeling guilty because you have failed once again? Why does this occur? How can you make "THIS TIME" different?

The reason most exercise programs fail is they are all or nothing approaches. You start a new exercise program with much enthusiasm, exercising every day. The first day you fail to exercise, you feel guilty, feel you failed and the program is terminated.

Most of us do not start an exercise regime simply for our health. It is our vanity that gets us moving. Feeling good and looking good is what it's all about. In a world where you must present yourself to others daily, it is important to look attractive and feel good. We all recognize that if we exercised daily our bodies and state of mind would improve. Why, then, don't we readily get off our well-padded rears and exercise?

Unfortunately, our vanity is usually balanced by another very powerful human characteristic, laziness. As much as we'd like to look sleek, there is another side to us that would rather drive around the parking lot for an hour than walk an extra block. Actually, this wonderful human characteristic, laziness, can be put to work *for* us rather than *against* us in the battle against corpulence. Instead of hating your laziness, *use it to your advantage.*

9

The first step is to realize you *are* lazy. Then you can plan to offset your tendency to not exercise by using some simple self-management techniques. You may say, "But I have no willpower to make myself do something that is against my nature." Willpower, however, isn't something you have or you don't. It is something to be learned. Another word for willpower is self-control. To teach yourself willpower or self-control, apply the following principle:

Make a high probability behavior, such as eating a chocolate chip cookie, *contingent* on performance of a low probability behavior, such as exercise.

In other words, you can set up a contract with yourself that states: *If* I exercise *then* I may eat, but try to make the exchange as specific as possible. For example, *If* I jog in place for three minutes *then* I may eat one chocolate chip cookie. The "contingency contract" is *never* stated (or used) the other way around. For example, the following contract is worthless: *If* I eat a chocolate chip cookie *then* I must jog in place for three minutes.

The key is, you are trying to manage your eating and exercise behaviors to make them work *for* you, not *against* you. Exercise is usually a low priority in a person's life. To make it a high priority you must make a contract (written or verbal) to do your exercise *before* you perform a behavior that is of high priority at the present, such as eating. Eventually exercise will become a higher priority while eating will become less of a priority.

Basically, the exercise management plan described above is positive reinforcement strategy: You reward yourself with something you want, for performing the appropriate behavior, exercising. What do you do about inappropriate behavior such as eating a piece of candy you didn't want? You punish yourself, right? WRONG! Inappropriate behaviors are to be ignored. DO NOT PUNISH YOURSELF! The more attention you pay to these unwanted behaviors the longer they will stay around. Instead, concentrate on the positive steps you make. If you learn to reward yourself for the appropriate behaviors—such as walking around the block instead of grabbing for the candy immediately—you will begin to feel better about yourself since you are taking positive steps toward learning self-control.

In exercise management, as in diet management, you are trying to shape your behavior slowly. That is, by taking small progressive steps you are trying to reach an ideal behavior. The mistake most people make is they try to do too much, too soon. They set themselves up for failure. Often people feel they must have a full hour in the day to exercise or it won't do them any good. Since most people don't feel they have an hour in the day they never get around to doing the exercise. When you are developing a new exercise habit you are trying to put it into your already action-packed day. So often I hear from people, "Exercise? Sure, I'd love to but I'm on the go from the minute I get up until I go to bed." How does a person learn to fit exercise into her daily lifestyle?

Vickie Vodon supervises the off-season conditioning program of one of her athletes.

If you try to shock your system by taking too big a step, such as an hour of daily exercise after starting from zero, eventually you will find yourself reacting with resistance. Imagine a houseguest who surprises you with a two-month visit compared to a one-hour visit. A one-hour visit you can adjust to more readily, while the two-month visit you may do everything in your power to get out of. It's just too big a commitment. If, however, the one-hour visit is fun, you may decide you want that visit to last longer. This would be a conscious decision on your part.

The message is to start small; you can always increase your exercise. Only you know how much exercise you have been doing consistently and how much you are capable of starting with.

To "Shape" your exercise behavior remember two points: (1) No exercise goal is too small and (2) No step upward in exercise is too small. As long as you are moving toward your final exercise goal, a new and better habit, *you should feel good about yourself.*

Do not make the mistake of dismissing a step as being too insignificant because it doesn't cause an immediate weight loss or immediate change in your body. It is the small changes that make the large changes over a lifetime! *It is not the exercise that matters, it is the development of a new and appropriate exercise habit that is the key.*

Thus, the basic plan for starting and maintaining an exercise habit has three major components: (1) Set a goal, one you are *sure* you can complete, (2) Complete your exercise goal and (3) Reward yourself. What you are trying to do in this exercise management plan is to set up your life to guarantee yourself success. DON'T CHEAT YOURSELF . . . make a contract, pairing exercise with a reinforcer, such as food, and keep it. Don't make your exercise goal so high that you set yourself up for failure. Start out by making the amount of exercise you must do to get your reward minimal then gradually make

the amount of exercise more. NOTHING SUCCEEDS LIKE SUCCESS!

Don't be embarrassed to reward yourself for exercising. You are learning to be good to yourself instead of punishing yourself. But only reward yourself after you have completed your exercise goals.

What if you aren't succeeding in completing the exercise goals you set out for yourself? Don't despair. These are not failures, rather they are nonsuccesses that can be corrected in the following way: If you aren't completing your goal then: (1) You have set your goal too high, therefore set a new lower goal, or (2) You haven't chosen a meaningful or strong enough reward, therefore you should change your reward or set a lower exercise goal.

How do you avoid the Oh-what-the-hell exercise syndrome? Everybody has good and bad days. Depression, fatigue, the blahs—any of these can and do occur. When they occur the urge to exercise is nonexistent.

If you are having a bad day then set a very low exercise goal and complete it. Any exercise is better than none. If you complete the low goal you should feel good about yourself . . . even if the goal was extremely small. Actually, if you do exercise on a bad day this often helps alleviate part of the bad feeling. You usually feel "extra" good about yourself. Why is this?

Each day you set goals that you want to accomplish. If you succeed in completing these goals you feel successful; that is, you feel good about yourself. In a day when everything else may have gone wrong, if you succeed in doing something for *you*—exercise—you feel you have accomplished something.

With a self-management approach to exercise, there is no need to terminate the exercise program if you fail to exercise for a day, a week, etc. This is not an all or nothing approach. This program allows for mistakes. We can't be perfect at all times. You are attempting to change habits. These habit changes take time.

Cellulite

by Dr. Anita Columbu (as told to Laura Mishima)

For most women, cellulite is a bad word. It implies ugly fat deposits, flabby skin and a low self-esteem to match. The strictly female problem is amplified by doctors—male medical doctors in particular—who like to pretend it doesn't exist.

As a doctor of chiropractic whose job involves observing bodies on a daily basis, I can honestly say that not only does cellulite exist, many women who are the right body weight have it. I believe that cellulite is a product of both junk-food eating habits and a sedentary lifestyle. I also believe that cellulite is caused in part by hormones, because men never seem to get it.

Why am I the expert on cellulite? At 5'2" and 108 pounds, it hardly seems likely that I should suffer from sagging skin. But cellulite is something I lived with for 20 years. I first noticed the problem as a 15-year-old teenager, and not until three years ago did I completely rid myself of this pesky flab. My fight against cellulite is a never-ending, conscious struggle.

Cellulite is a combination of fat, toxic accumulation, fluid and lack of muscle tone. It is particularly prevalent in the United States, where most women don't walk. For 12 years, we sit in the classroom while our bodies are developing.

Lunges performed by Stacey Bentley.

Then it's either college (more sitting), a desk job (most women have sedentary jobs), or marriage and motherhood. We drive or ride everywhere. The American society is geared towards automation and TV-viewing—let someone else exert the effort for you.

What a contrast to the lifestyle in Sardinia, where Franco's sisters climb up and down mountains ten times a day to get water from the center of town. I have never seen such beautiful, thin, well-defined, muscular bodies on nonathletic women.

One reason is exercise and the other is nutrition. In Sardinia, there is less refined food. Fast-food temptations are nonexistent. Proper nutrition is more than half the battle against cellulite and most common American diseases.

What causes *cellulite?*

1. Lack of exercise.
2. Refined foods.
3. Chemicals, preservatives, additives, toxins and poisons, such as drugs and tobacco.
4. Hormonal imbalance.

Cellulite's favorite hideouts are the back thigh, hips, stomach and sometimes back arm. As I stated earlier, you need not be overweight to get it. The tendency begins in puberty, and if you are inactive, your tendency is greater. If you're involved in athletics, cellulite may be less visible, but you may still get it for the above reasons.

There are two kinds of cellulite: hard and soft. *Hard cellulite* appears on women who are overweight. Their fatty deposits are more packed in, so the cellulite must be broken down by deep massage. You may try self-massage or seek

Squats

a professional who can work areas which are hard to reach. The idea is to get the blood circulating to these areas.

Once you have surpassed this stage, you have *soft cellulite*—my problem for twenty years. If you are close to your normal weight but find loose, hanging bulges in the aforementioned areas, you have soft cellulite.

There are two ways to fight it: further *vigorous massage* with a product like the Weider Slimmer's Glove while bathing to increase circulation and *high-repetition exercises* with light weight or no weight. The French glove is most effective once the muscles have tightened through consistent exercise.

My problem with cellulite was due to the fact that I gained and lost weight for many years. When I gained, the weight would go straight to my hips and thighs (I weighed as much as 135 pounds). The tissue became stretched and when I lost, I wouldn't exercise.

Lying Rear Leg Lifts

My solution was high-repetition exercises for the legs, thighs, hips and stomach. Any exercise done properly will help tone and reduce these areas. My repertoire includes half-squats, jumping rope and running. I also use ankle weights to perform side leg raises, donkey kicks, back leg raises and other leg exercises (as illustrated in our women's weight training book, *Starbodies*). I'm sure you can innovate and add to my list.

The important thing to concentrate on is lifting and flexing. Be in complete control of the movement and avoid using momentum. Lift from the hip—don't throw your leg—and emphasize tightening the buttocks.

I believe that cellulite can be eliminated if you

are willing to give a constant commitment and work at it every day. At 32 years of age, I eliminated it for the first time. I am convinced that the body will respond at any age!

Free-Hand Lunges

The next phase of my cellulite prevention program is nutrition. Eliminating cellulite involves both exercise and nutrition. One of my vices was drinking two or three cups of coffee daily. Caffeine is a poison—it is bad for the nervous system, causing tension, irritability and yes, cellulite. It traps the poison in cells.

The American public must learn to read labels and avoid preservatives, additives and chemicals. What I am asking takes time, but most women don't think twice about the hours they spend at a beauty salon with hairdressers, manicures and facials. If you are healthy and free of cellulite, your body will radiate not only beauty but health.

Another problem we face is meat grown with hormones. This has a direct effect on your body and can cause your own hormonal balance to be upset—especially for women taking the pill or those with an endocrine imbalance. The same logic verifies my statement that cellulite is in part caused by estrogen, the female hormone. From my experience at the office, men—regardless of obesity—never get it.

One way to flush these toxins out of the body is by drinking eight to 10 glasses of water daily. Our bodies suffer from both automobile intoxication and food poisons. Most women fail to drink the recommended amount of water each day for fear of water retention and

bloating. That's a big mistake.

While I don't recommend diuretics, which disturb one's electrolyte balance and cause too much potassium to be excreted, I do recommend a number of natural diuretics: apple juice, cranberry juice and vitamin B_6.

Otherwise, eat mostly fresh fish. You may allow yourself fowl or beef without chemicals twice a week, plus the following dairy products: eggs (fertile), yogurt, cheese and milk (raw and unpasteurized, if available). Fresh fruits and vegetables (preferably raw) should be consumed daily.

Learn to enjoy fresh food, using lemon juice and herbs for seasoning. Eliminate all the extras—ketchup, mayonnaise, sugar and salad dressing. Salt causes fluid retention, and, along with sugar and fats (oils), is hidden in almost all the foods we buy. Again, learn to read labels.

Finally, you must practice relaxation techniques. All of us face a variety of stresses and tension each day, so it is important to

Kneeling Jazz Kicks

engage in some form of daily meditation. Visualize your body and how you want to look. Relax your mind and zero in on what you want to accomplish. Keep your goal very clear.

I have never met a person, male or female, including bodybuilding stars, who was 100 percent happy with his body. While there is no such thing as a perfect body, women in particular tend to *hate* a certain body part—either it is too small or too big.

My idea is to cleanse your mind of negative thought and stop demeaning yourself. Praise your good points, concentrate on improving weaknesses and watch that cellulite disappear!

Intensity Training for Figure Shaping

by Betty Weider

It's no secret that women all over the country are discovering the benefits of weight training.

New members are flocking to health clubs, gyms and spas in such numbers that the influx rivals the tennis boom of a few years ago—and the majority of these newcomers are women. The daytime television talk shows, whose audiences consist largely of women, are constantly booking experts on progressive resistance training as guests to give exercise instruction and advice. Even *Vogue* magazine is running an article by Arnold Schwarzenegger on weight training for women.

But, sadly, a lot of well-meaning effort is going to waste, and too many women are finding that they're simply not getting the results from their training that they anticipated. Disappointment usually leads to disillusionment, and frequently the individual simply stops trying.

Why this wasted effort? According to a lot of experts, it's mostly because so many women have misconceptions about how their bodies work, and what it takes to cause the changes they'd like to make in their physiques. Hard work alone isn't enough. If you want to shape up, firm up, burn fat and get strong, you simply have to master the proper techniques.

"It breaks my heart to see the way women are taught to train at most health clubs," says Cathy Gelfo. Cathy is Mike Mentzer's fianceé and business partner, General Secretary of the Women's Committee of the IFBB, and very involved, herself, with weight training. "They think that just by going through the motions, they're going to be able to shape themselves up. But it just doesn't work that way."

Cathy believes there are two basic areas in weight training where a lot of women lack understanding:

1. They don't know the proper techniques of training, nor comprehend why those techniques are important.
2. They don't approach their training with sufficient intensity.

A fundamental difficulty, she has observed, comes from the fact that many women have very little understanding of their own bodies. They're weak, but they don't see this weakness because they were never taught to appreciate their own inherent strength or to think that developing this strength was desirable. Along with this, they were never expected to be physically competent.

No disgrace was attached to their being unable to lift and carry, use a screwdriver or hammer a nail. So it should come as no surprise that learning to do a Bench Press or Barbell Curl properly could present difficulties.

"I was fortunate," Cathy explains. "I grew up in a household with an athletic father and brothers, so I always used my strength without thinking about it. My sister and I still arm wrestle for fun, just like we did when we were growing up. The idea never occurred to us that a woman had to be weak to be feminine. Nonsense."

Cathy is concerned about women developing their natural strength potential for more reasons than just how they look and feel. She points to the number of times a woman is on her own, having to look out for herself, carry her own groceries. When that happens, she just can't depend on having a man hanging around to help her.

"Look at all the cases where a woman is married 10–15 years, and suddenly gets divorced and has to go to work and look out for herself. The result can be tragic unless she makes up her mind to be independent."

But Cathy also points to more mundane circumstances, such as what happened to her when she flew to Philadelphia in August to meet her fiancé at the Ms. Olympia contest.

"I had a suitcase full of Mike's courses, tapes and T-shirts that we were going to sell at the show, and I swear it must have weighed 200 pounds. Most of the time I had to carry it by myself. In Philadelphia I asked a porter to load it onto the bus at the airport, and he hefted it once and shook his head. *I* had to put it on myself."

Cathy says she owes her strength to the fact that she trains hard and correctly. Of course, having Mr. Universe as coach is a great advantage. But Cathy had already taken up weight training at the University of Maryland in 1975 just before she met Mike. Through his guidance, she learned to get much more from her efforts in the gym, and to get results in short periods of training, a condition necessitated by her busy schedule.

"Most people don't have much time to train," she says. "That's why intensity training is so valuable. Instead of having to spend hours a day at your workout, you can get in and out of the gym with even better results."

Aware that most women don't know how to train intensely or why this kind of workout is so valuable, Mike and Cathy have written a booklet

Mike Mentzer (Mr. Universe) spots Cathy Gelfo for a heavy set of Squats.

called "Heavy Duty For Women" to explain the advantages of intensity training.

"The whole idea of Heavy Duty training is simply that the muscles of the body won't respond unless they're subjected to a significant overload," says Cathy. "So doing 30 or 40 reps with a light weight won't accomplish anything except increase your endurance. You have to ask the muscles to do something almost impossible; otherwise why should they adapt? So there is no such thing as heavy or light training—there's only training as hard as you can. That's as true for women as it is for men. It's based on the nature of muscle, and women's muscles are physiologically the same as men's."

The proper way to do a set, or group of repetitions, Cathy explains, is to choose a weight that lets you do 6–10 reps. Then do as many reps as you possibly can. Don't stop just because you've reached a certain number. If you can do more than 10 reps, you should be using a slightly heavier weight; if you can't do at least six, switch to one a little lighter.

"A lot of women go into a gym to shape up and firm up their figures," Cathy says. "And they're afraid of building large muscles. They talk about developing muscle 'tone,' although I don't know exactly what that's supposed to be. The

fact is, if they don't train hard and heavy enough, they won't get any results at all. And that's a terrible waste of time and effort."

"When a woman goes on a really strict diet and loses a lot of body fat," adds Mike Mentzer, "the muscle revealed underneath is generally stringy and lacks shape. That's because it lacks mass. If you want to give your body real shape and develop its natural contours, that means you need additional mass."

Mike points out that women lack the proper hormones to add mass easily. Therefore, just adding sufficient mass to give their bodies an attractive shape requires hard, intense workouts. The fears many women have of developing unattractive bulk, he says, are groundless.

"They should live so long," he says with a smile. "I've dedicated myself to bodybuilding since I was twelve years old, and I seem to have the genetic potential for muscle. But it has taken me all this time. If some woman discovers a way to pack on muscle bulk in a few months at a health spa, I wish she'd tell me."

Heavy Duty training, according to Cathy and Mike, is based on the idea that you can work hard or you can work long, but you can't do both simultaneously—in the same way that a runner can go all out in a sprint, but can't expect to continue like that much more than 100 yards, while a marathon runner can keep going for hours as long as he paces himself carefully.

"Building the body requires intensive effort, not long workouts," Cathy explains. "You work as hard as you can for as long as you can. You don't pace yourself at all. When you pace yourself, you lose intensity. And you don't send the right signals to the muscles. You have to overload them, not give them a chance to get by with what they can already do."

Intensity, as Cathy and Mike define it, can be achieved in several ways:

1. Lifting more weight in a given period.
2. Doing more sets in a given period.
3. Doing the same amount of work in shorter and shorter periods.

Obviously, if you're already lifting as much weight as you can—reaching a point of failure at 10 repetitions—you can't add more weight to the exercises. Mike has some techniques for using more weight and the assistance of a workout partner to increase intensity. But these techniques are more for advanced bodybuilders than beginners.

Cathy Gelfo and her training partner vividly illustrate the tremendous intensity women are capable of putting into their weight workouts. The weight room is no longer exclusively a man's world!

Doing more sets can have its advantages, but once again you run into the problem of the sprinter—if you're working to your limit, which you should be in progressive resistance training, you shouldn't be able to do any more.

The third way, gradually diminishing the time it takes to get through a specified workout, has practical advantages. It never requires that you do more than you actually can, only that you do it with less rest between sets. And it gets you out of the gym that much faster.

"I know I'd get bored if I had to spend hours in the gym," Cathy says, "and I wouldn't have that kind of time anyway. But when I know I only have to train for 40 or 50 minutes at most, and that that time will gradually become less and less, I know I can always get in my workouts no matter how busy I am."

There's a big difference between working steadily for this amount of time, and just sort of hanging around the gym, doing a set here, a set there, talking to your friends, and never raising a sweat, Mike Mentzer points out.

"It requires concentration. And, once you get through it, you need time to recuperate. My own workouts have gotten so intense that I can't train more than three times a week. In fact, recuperation is a good measure of how hard you've really worked. If you recuperate too quickly, you know you've been doing something wrong."

All this talk of hard training, intensity and the rest, Cathy Gelfo realizes, may seem alien to a lot of women. But that, she says, is all the more reason they have to be made aware of how progressive resistance training really works, and what it can do for them.

"It's accepted nowadays that women can be doctors and lawyers," she says. "Why is it so strange that they should develop their bodies as well as their minds? Who says that real femininity is achieved by visits to the beauty parlor? Let's discover the natural beauty of the body instead of relying on cosmetics."

You don't have to train at Gold's Gym in order to have a good workout, she adds, but you can't necessarily rely on what you are told by $3.50-an-hour "instructors" in a lot of spas. You have to set your own pace, develop your own standards, and establish your own personal goals.

In their booklet, Cathy and Mike offer complete workouts for beginner, intermediate and advanced weight trainers. But here are a few basic suggestions they believe will enhance your workouts.

When training very heavily, it's essential to have a training partner. She can spot you in heavy lifts, help you to complete forced reps, and offer vital encouragement when the going gets tough.

1. Choose a weight for each exercise that lets you do 6–10 reps.
2. The last rep you do should be the last possible rep you can do.
3. Work for the fullest range of movement in each exercise—from full extension to full contraction of the muscle.
4. Make the muscle work throughout the exercise. Don't let the weight swing up or drop down. Control the weight with the muscle.
5. Train at a deliberate pace. Don't go so quickly that you overtax your cardiovascular system.
6. As a general rule, train the bigger muscles of the body before you work the smaller ones.
7. Rest the minimum possible time between sets.
8. To further increase intensity, gradually diminish rest time between sets.
9. Give yourself enough time to recuperate. This will usually be a minimum of 48 hours for any given muscle group, and sometimes longer if your training has gotten really intense.
10. Don't rely on weight training to burn up calories. If you want to lose fat, moderate your diet, and include some low-intensity/high-reptition exercise in your program. Jogging, riding a bicycle and swimming are excellent for this. Walking is also an ideal calorie-consumer.
11. Warm up before you train, but do just enough to prevent injury, since more will cut down on your ability to train intensely.

"You don't have to want to be a competition bodybuilder to learn how to really build up your body," Cathy says. "But you must realize that if you don't train full out, you won't get maximum results. As for me, I want to become just as strong and developed as I possibly can. And I don't worry that this will make me less feminine. On the contrary, I believe it makes me that much more attractive. If you don't believe me, ask Mike."

Why I Train with Men

by Claudia Wilbourn

A lot of people have asked me why I prefer to work out exclusively with men. The answer is simply that I need a training partner who's capable of pushing me, trains as hard as I do and is really serious about making progress. Except for a handful of other women bodybuilders, that leaves me with no choice of workout partners except men.

I've instructed women for years and have worked out with them. Most of them just don't train very hard. They tend to stop when they feel any pain at all. But that's precisely the time when you need to push hard to make any real gains. When you have a workout partner who doesn't push, it's hard for you to keep pushing.

When I train with a man, I think both of us benefit. It inspires me to work as hard as I can. But the man gets something out of it, too. Men want to look the best they can, and they will often push harder when they're training with a woman. Plus, they don't get involved with the competitive thing that they might with another man. For one thing, I can't lift as much weight as a good male bodybuilder. But the name of the game in bodybuilding is lifting enough weight to shape your body. It's not a weightlifting contest.

Of course, men are always surprised at how hard I train. I'll push just as hard as the man, and they aren't ready for that. They're also surprised at how strong I am—and how serious. I like a good time as well as anyone, but in the gym all that counts is training, and I concentrate totally on the workout.

But a lot of traditionalistic men are put off by this. They say my attitude is "unfeminine." I guess they're thinking about the "spa ladies" or something, because all good women athletes nowadays have to train 100 percent to have a chance at winning. The competition is just as tough for us as it is for the men. Watch any college women's basketball team working out, or women track-and-field athletes trying to make the Olympics, and you'll find the same attitude.

But at least those women have a place to train. Many bodybuilding gyms won't let me in the door. That's why I come up to Gold's Gym a lot all the way from Orange County—Pete Grymkowski and the guys at Gold's have always been supportive. Now that people have begun to hear about me, a few other bodybuilding gyms have welcomed me. But this attitude certainly isn't universal.

Many gym owners tell me, "We don't want you to train here because you might upset the

Andreas Cahling (Mr. International) urges Claudia Wilbourn to complete a few extra presses on a Universal Gym machine.

men.'' I don't know what they mean, exactly. Maybe they expect me to train in a bikini and go prancing around nude in the men's locker room. Actually, the only way I would upset the men in a lot of gyms is by showing them up.

I think good gyms ought to welcome serious bodybuilders—whether they're male or female— and take a more critical stance toward people who just make a nuisance of themselves. I know it bugs me when I'm training really hard and have to stop because some idiot is monopolizing the equipment. You know, the kind that does a set of Bench Presses, and then lies there on the bench to recuperate. Man or woman, I don't like to see that. Jump in, do your set, and get on with it. That's the only way.

Even when I'm allowed to train in gyms, I still get a lot of criticism. Like people make fun of me when I grunt and groan doing a heavy exercise. I just go over and tell them, "Hey, I'm lifting twice my body weight over there. You think you can do the same?" That usually shuts them up.

And then there are the rumors I keep hearing about myself, how I'm really masculine, take a lot of steroids, or that I'm a lesbian or something. I just can't be bothered by things like that. Men have had to put up with that kind of thing for a long time, so I guess I can't expect to be immune. The thing is, since male bodybuilders know what it's like to be criticized by a lot of ignorant people who have no idea what you're trying to accomplish, you'd think they'd be more supportive. Some are, but a lot aren't.

I can go into Gold's and train with my friend Kurt Shull, or with somebody like Andreas

Cahling, and everything's fine. Most of the people at Gold's are real advocates of women's bodybuilding. But then I go to a contest and in the scoring I'm placed behind two dancers who have never lifted weights. I go to another competition and find that I'll be disqualified if I do any poses that show off the muscular development I've worked so hard to achieve.

One contest I was in recently was a disaster. I heard later that one of the judges, who happens to be a really second-rate bodybuilder who never won anything, gave me a very low score because he said, "Oh, I think she's gone too far."

What does that mean? Did anyone ever tell

In endurance movements like Roman Chair Sit-ups, Andreas and Claudia are evenly matched.

Arnold or Zane or Mentzer that they "went too far?" Tell me that I lack symmetry or proportion or muscularity—basic elements in the judging of bodybuilding—but not that business of going too far, which means, I guess, that the guy thought he was judging some kind of beauty contest and my physique didn't turn him on.

But none of that kind of thing is going to discourage me from continuing to work at perfecting my physique. And the only way I know how to do that is to train with the best partner available, and that is usually going to be a man. All I have to worry about is training intensely enough so that I am the best training partner the guy can find. It works both ways.

Incidentally, for all those people who still don't believe in men and women as training partners, I'd like to point out that Frank Zane won his third Olympia after training every night in Gold's with his wife Christine. If a woman training partner is good enough for Mr. Olympia, I think that should end the argument.

When women have male training partners, they notice that the man's superior strength pushes them to greater efforts. On the other hand, a woman's generally greater endurance forces the man to do longer workouts.

How to Use a Gym

by Betty Weider

Women in increasing numbers are discovering the health and appearance benefits of weight training. But for every one who has made this discovery, there are hundreds, I'm afraid, who are still in the dark.

"Betty," Susan Tiffany tells me, "when I hear some of the questions women ask in the gym, some of the things they believe about their bodies, I could just about break down and cry."

Susan is a dancer, actress and model who found herself spending so much time in the gym that she decided she ought to be paid for it. Currently, she's managing the women's gym at the Sports Connection in Beverly Hills, Calif. Working in that kind of place, she believes, has given her real insight into the problems women face when they try to use a gym.

"We get all kinds of women here," she says. "A lot of famous actresses and models, as well as professional women, housewives and secretaries. Some of them know what they're doing, but an awful lot of them don't."

Susan feels that women have a lot of misconceptions about training that can seriously interfere with progress. Basically, these misconceptions fall into three categories:

1. How the body reacts to various kinds of exercise.
2. How progressive-resistance training works.
3. How to use a gym.

"Women usually understand cardiovascular and flexibility training," Susan explains. "But a lot of them have no idea what to do about their muscles."

A lot of women come into a gym and want to slenderize and firm up their bodies. To them, this means losing fat without gaining any muscle mass. They are terrified of getting bulky.

"It's difficult sometimes to get them to train with weights at all," says Susan, "because they think they're going to end up with arms like Arnold Schwarzenegger. They don't understand the relationship between muscles and shape."

Women, Susan has observed, rely mostly on diet to get more slender, and they think of gym training as a way of hurrying this calorie-burning process. What they don't realize is that getting rid of body fat is just going to expose stringy, shapeless and unattractive muscles unless they do some sort of training to improve muscular shape.

Only in large commercial gyms can you find a variety of equipment wide enough to allow optimum workouts.

"Shape is mass," Susan says. "That's where those lovely contours in a dancer's legs come from—you can't have shape unless there's something there to be shaped. But the chances of women developing so much mass that they look bulky and unaesthetic are just about nil."

Actually, many women need more muscle mass than they have, but they aren't aware of this fact because their bodies are covered with an extra layer of fat. They would profit by losing an inch of adipose tissue and replacing it with a half inch of muscle tissue. You can shape and contour muscle, but fat just sits there.

"I usually explain to women that it takes an abundance of male hormone to produce huge amounts of muscle mass," Susan says, "and that most of the men who train with weights are working their tails off to get bigger—and not too many of them are making rapid progress. If it's so hard for the men, I point out, why should the women expect to get faster results with less genetic capability?"

The first step for women in understanding how to train is to realize they have the same skeletal muscles that men do, and to accept the fact that these muscles need to be exercised to produce a really shapely and firm figure. The question then is: how? And that's where progressive-resistance training comes into the equation.

"I usually start the women on Nautilus or Universal machines," Susan explains, "because that way they don't have to coordinate and balance free weights. But a lot of them expect the machines to do the work. One even suggested we put a *motor* on a Nautilus pullover machine so that she could do more reps at a time. The idea of progressive-resistance training is foreign to a lot of them."

Muscles, as most *Muscle & Fitness* readers know, adapt when you put unaccustomed stresses on them. Keep working them against greater resistance, and they continue to get stronger, firmer and shapelier. If you don't continue to increase the amount of resistance, the muscles never develop any further.

"After we start the women out on a program,"

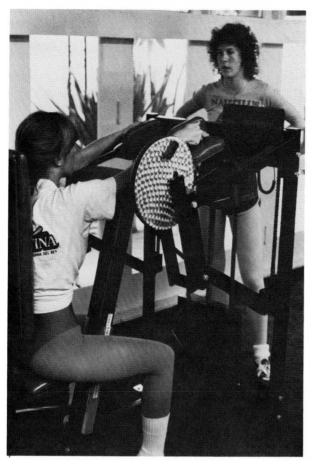

Nautilus clubs have sprung up all over America, but few of them also have free-weight equipment.

face, but when they see a star, a beautiful woman they really admire, training with the kind of intensity they would expect from a man, that brings the point home: women look that way because they work at it. They suddenly realize that beauty is maintained by a lot of sweat and effort, and you don't get something for nothing."

Persuading women to train hard is obviously the first, and biggest, challenge. The next challenge, says Susan, is getting them to train all parts of the body equally.

"Most women act as if they had no muscles above the waist except the pectorals," she says. "They train legs really hard, doing Lunges, Leg Extensions, Side Leg Raises. And they do a lot of abdominal work. But the only muscles above the waist they're concerned about are the pectorals, to firm up the bustline."

Susan makes sure to include exercises for the shoulders, back and arms in the routines she

Health spas offer access to a wide variety of exercise machines as well as to free weights.

Susan tells me, "we check them periodically. An amazing number of them never increase the amount of weight they are using unless we do it for them."

Teaching women that they ought to be using as much weight as they can is one of the toughest things about Susan's job.

"They just don't want to strain,' she says. "Most of them have never really used their muscles in their entire lives. The basic concept of hard muscular work is alien to them.

"As Joe Weider always told Arnold Schwarzenegger and the other champions he helped develop, 'No pain, no gain.' Maybe that epigram should be on the wall of every women's gym in the country."

Susan has more delicate ways of getting this message across, and she has found allies in the lovely actresses and models who train at the Beverly Hills gym.

"It helps if I can point to a famous television actress who is really working hard, lifting heavy weights. You can explain until you're blue in the

Arnold Schwarzenegger supervises the workouts of two acquaintances.

prepares for the women. As mentioned earlier, she has the women do most of the exercises on machines because women accept them more readily than free weights. But she urges them to use free weights when training the arms. She finds free weights work much better than the various arm machines.

"The way to get women to follow a fully balanced routine," Susan says, "is to base the workouts on circuit training. I think that works better for most women than doing a number of sets in a row for the same body part."

In circuit training you do a single set of an exercise for each body part, one body part after another, with no rest between exercises, until you have completed a full circuit. At this point, you can do a second complete circuit, which may or may not include the same exercises that you did in the first.

Circuit training ensures that you work the whole body equally. And since you're giving each muscle group time to recover before you train it again, you can keep working rapidly enough, without pausing between exercises, to burn up the maximum number of calories. Still another advantage is that circuit training doesn't resemble traditional "weightlifting" routines, so it doesn't set off a lot of women's prejudices.

"Of course, I'm making generalizations when I describe the way women train," says Susan. "A lot of them come into the gym and attack the equipment. It differs from gym to gym. Over at the Santa Monica Sports Connection, women are allowed to use the men's gym, and when you get men and women training together, the women train with a lot more intensity. It makes the men do their best, too. Also, the women at Santa Monica tend to be a bit younger, and younger women usually train harder."

I asked Susan if she could give me a simple checklist of things women should know to get the most out of their weight training. This is what she came up with:

1. Women's muscles get bigger with training, but not much bigger.
2. Muscle mass in women usually produces improvement in shape, which means a better, more curvaceous figure.
3. You burn off fat to show the muscle underneath; fat does not *ever* turn into muscle.
4. If you get through your set of repetitions too easily (say, you could have done 3–5 more), you should be training with more weight. No pain, no gain.

5. Machines and free weights do basically the same thing: they provide resistance against which your muscles can contract. One type of equipment doesn't automatically make you bigger, and the other type more slender.
6. Free weights (barbells and dumbbells) feel different to use than machines. You have to experiment to see what suits you for any given exercise.
7. In most cases the upper body is relatively less developed than the lower body. Therefore, it requires a lot more training.
8. The biggest changes in the body take the longest time; exercise helps control weight, but not in the absence of diet. Don't expect overnight changes in the body.
9. Progressive-resistance training is not enough; you need aerobic and flexibility training as well.

"It's easiest to sell weight training to women on the basis of how it makes you healthier, better-looking and sexier—because it does," Susan points out. "But there's another point that I emphasize. The idea that women should be weak and helpless is, I believe, a bad one. We aren't Victorians. A woman can't depend on the fact that there will always be a man around to help her. I think she should discover her own physical potential, just as she discovers the potential of her other talents and abilities. I think

Seated Pulley Rowing tones the back muscles and improves shoulder posture.

it's a crime if you can't even carry your own bag of groceries or a suitcase. What do you do if you really need to? And who said women were supposed to develop into physical cripples? That doesn't make any sense to me."

Strength and femininity are not mutually exclusive. A woman can be both strong and sexy. And training the body becomes more important rather than less important with age. When a woman doesn't subject her body to resistance training, the muscles begin to sag and atrophy as early as age 22. By the age of 30 or 40, it's possible for a woman to lose all the sex appeal that she was so proud of when she was younger.

But firming and toning the body with weight training can slow down, and in some cases even reverse, what age and gravity inflict on the body. And the sooner you get to a gym and start a training program, the sooner you can expect some results.

"When I say that a lot of the women who come to the gym are ignorant about training," Susan concludes, "I don't mean to put them down. They've been fed a lot of false information in the books and magazines they have read all their lives, and yet here they are coming into a gym anyway. That takes guts. And once they get over their initial prejudices and see what kind of results they can get from progressive-resistance workouts, they become dedicated to training. Ignorant, at first, maybe— but they catch on quick."

Shaping Up with Running, Jogging, and Walking

by Betty Weider

Somebody once wrote a futuristic science-fiction story about a society in which people had become so accustomed to going around in wheeled vehicles that their legs had virtually atrophied. Instead of walking, these pople moved about in little electric carts. When they wanted to go longer distances, they wheeled these carts into larger vehicles and sped to their destinations in these.

I'm sure the author was trying to make a point. Oh, we still have legs. But how many of us get into the car and drive a few blocks when we could easily walk? Or, on another level, how many past the age of 20 are still in good enough condition to run five miles or more? Sadly, the answer is not very many.

Evolution just never counted on the internal combustion engine. The forces of nature took millions of years preparing us for two-legged, upright locomotion, a means of mobility that let early man stand up and look over the tall grass to spot his enemies, and freed his hands to make and use tools. Well, our needs have obviously changed. But here is the problem: it has become apparent that our entire physiological and psychological makeup is, to some extent, dependent on this kind of physical activity and the whole system gets in trouble without it.

Of course, a few people are beginning to catch on. We hear and read reports about runners who experience a kind of "high" when they exercise over a period of time. And it has become apparent that running, jogging and even walking can be decisive in long-term weight control. There is even some evidence that running can be a depression-fighter that works even better than medication for some people!

No one thing is a total cure-all, but getting out there and using your two legs seems to have benefits that just can't be ignored. So I'd like to take this time to examine some of these benefits, and to look at some ways of including this type of exercise in your own personal bodybuilding program.

RUNNING AND THE HEART

It's important to note that the heart is a muscle. It gets bigger and stronger through exercise. A stronger heart beats a lot slower, so it lasts longer. So how do you go about exercising your heart?

Simple. Any activity that gets your heart and pulse rate up to 120–140 beats or more a minute,

Lynn Conkwright, World Bodybuilding Champion, regularly enjoys a relaxing run on the beach as part of her aerobic conditioning program.

and keeps it there for 12 to 15 minutes, strengthens your heart. It also improves the efficiency of the lungs and circulatory system in getting oxygen to the muscles. Six weeks or so of this kind of exercise gets you "in shape," and enables you to keep up the activity for extended periods of time.

You can achieve this type of condition in various ways—through swimming, jumping rope, riding a bicycle, and running. Of these methods, running seems to have become the most popular. There is something so basic, so natural to running that people seem to prefer it to other cardiovascular activities by a wide margin. And, in addition to getting you into shape, running for extended periods of time seems to have numerous fringe benefits.

THE PSYCHOLOGY OF RUNNING

When you go out for a run, the first 20 minutes or so can be uncomfortable. Most people feel stiff, slow, and the symptoms of anxiety and depression seem to increase. This turns a lot of people off, and they never get any further with their running program.

Ah, but if you can continue your running so

you're out longer than 20 minutes, if you keep going past the initial barrier, something else is likely to happen. They call it the "runner's high," and there are disagreements as to what causes it. The senses become more alert. Feelings of fatigue, depression and anxiety go away. The whole body seems to work better, feel stronger, and the world becomes a better, brighter place in which to live.

There are a number of possible explanations for this phenomenon. One concerns brain chemistry. In manic-depressive illness, patients in the depressed state show a marked decrease in a neurotransmitter called *norepinephrine*. When they are manic, the situation is reversed. The studies aren't complete as yet, but there is some reason to believe that running increases the brain's production of this chemical, which would account for the runner's tremendous shift of mood.

But there are other possibilities. For one, running results in a significant loss of salt from the body. If you examine the effects of lithium, a drug that is highly effective in the treatment of depression, you find that it drives salt out of the cells by replacing the sodium ion with a lithium ion. Could running be a natural means of getting

Ms. Conkwright has discovered that running also accelerates her metabolism, making it easier to keep off excess body fat.

the effects of lithium without the necessity of any medication?

And there are other effects. Running changes the levels of glucose, testosterone and other biochemical compounds that are associated with anxiety, depression and aggression. But whatever the specific causes of the "runner's high" and other changes in the psychology of the runner, it seems apparent that this kind of exercise helps us govern our moods and control stress. Only our modern, sedentary lifestyle may have caused us to forget about our needs in this area, so that we've been suffering the consequences without realizing why.

RUNNING AND WEIGHT CONTROL

When you run a mile you use up about 100 calories. This doesn't seem like much—a tablespoon of butter, after all, contains the same amount. But that expenditure of calories can actually be quite significant when it occurs daily over a period of time.

Figure it this way: running one mile a day, five days a week, over a period of a year works out like this—100 calories × 5 days × 52 weeks = 26,000 calories. A pound of fat is equal to about

3500 calories. Therefore, over the course of the year, an expenditure of 26,000 calories is equivalent to: 26,000 ÷ 3500 = 7.4 pounds.

Now it's a fact that very few people who are motivated enough to run a mile five times a week are going to stop at that distance. Soon they will be running five miles or more, and then you are talking about 20–30 pounds or more in equivalent caloric expenditure. And that's without doing anything about dieting!

But there is another way in which running helps us control our weight. Most of us don't do enough exercise to notice, but it seems that our bodies have some sort of appetite thermostat that is activated by extensive activity.

When we don't exercise much, our appetites and our actual need for food don't seem to be very well coordinated. But when we run for exercise strenuously, something happens. The thermostat kicks in and we tend to eat about what we need and no more. Maybe it's because of those physiological changes I noted above, or it could be something entirely separate. Whatever it is, it works.

Runners don't stay slim just because they burn up a lot of energy. They actually eat more appropriate amounts of food than the rest of us.

STARTING A RUNNING PROGRAM

Starting to run when you are out of shape can be sheer misery if you don't go about it the right way. The thing is to start out slow, increase your activity a little at a time, and be patient. But once you get started, keep at it. Whenever you stop, even for a few days, you will find you have to practically start all over again.

For those of you who already exercise quite a bit, you may run into a different sort of problem when you start running. Probably, in a matter of a few days to a week, because of your previous conditioning, you will be able to take off and go for three to five miles or more. All well and good, but there's a catch.

Your previous training has not been specific to running. Sure, your lungs adapt quickly, but not your legs. They have to take up the shock of your entire weight with each step. As a result, it is very easy for you to outrun the capacity of your legs to withstand that kind of jarring. That means developing shin splints and other injuries, and setting back your running program by weeks or months.

So don't let your ego run away with you. Take it slow, and give your body a few weeks to adapt to this special kind of effort.

There are numerous publications on the market that go into (endless) detail on running techniques and accessories. All you really need, however, is a good pair of shoes and a place to run. That place should be away from the exhaust pipes of cars, and it helps if you run on softer surfaces like dirt or grass rather than concrete.

Women may want to consider wearing a bra while running, even if they normally do without one. Pectoral muscles are also subject to a great deal of trauma when you run. Smaller breasted women may find they can do without this support, and if there is no discomfort, there's probably no danger.

WALKING: THE MOST UNDERRATED EXERCISE

With all the emphasis that has been placed on running in the past few years, walking has been overlooked to some degree, and it's a shame. Consider this for a minute: when you propel yourself over a distance by means of your own legs and feet, no matter how fast or slow you go, you use approximately the same number of calories. Run a mile, walk a mile—in either case, you're using the same 100 calories. You just use them faster when you run.

Running and playing on the beach with a boyfriend can build great fitness quite enjoyably.

Steve Reeves has been advocating walking as part of an exercise program for years. He is not alone. If you walk fast, you get some cardiovascular benefit, and you avoid any trauma to the legs and body. This means that the elderly or those with some physical ailments can walk for health, when they would not be able to run. And a half-hour walk a day can account for many pounds over the course of a year or so.

Walking is also a nice way to see the world. Whether it's walking in the woods, along the beach, or just exploring parts of your city—it's something you can do with the whole family, and it doesn't cost an arm and a leg.

YOU'RE ENTITLED!

Keep in mind while you are planning your own running, jogging or walking program that these benefits of health, happiness, weight and figure control are not just promises made by some purveyor of a new exercise "secret." They are things Mother Nature meant for us to have—assuming we go ahead and use our bodies in the manner Mother Nature intended.

You are not getting something for nothing: you are getting what you deserve. Enjoy it, you're entitled!

The Art of Posing

by Claudia Wilbourn

There was an air of expectancy in the audience that night. Most of the people had never seen a women's bodybuilding contest before, and they didn't really know what was going to happen. The trouble was, neither did I.

The 1979 Women's World Bodybuilding Championship, presented by Gold's Gym, was not only the first contest I entered—it was the first I had ever seen! Not that I was a newcomer to bodybuilding. I had been training very hard for a long time. I had a good physique, and I knew it. The problem was, how was I going to show it off to the audience?

I had never seen another woman pose. I had no idea of what Lisa Lyon, Stacey Bentley and the other contestants were going to do onstage. This was the beginning, after all. There had been other contests, but women's bodybuilding as a national sport was just getting off the ground. We were inventing it as we went along, not just those of us in the Gold's contest, but all the other women bodybuilders training from Florida to Washington, Maine to California. We had no models on whom to pattern ourselves.

Posing. I had not given it enough thought. And so I approached it the only way I knew—I used the poses I had seen my male bodybuilder

Once severely underweight, Claudia Wilbourn used bodybuilding to normalize her weight and improve her self-confidence.

33

friends use. Bodybuilding was bodybuilding, I reasoned. I failed to perceive that what was appropriate for the male bodybuilders might not be for the women. I had not yet begun to understand that posing is much more than simply showing the body; it's a truly creative art in which the personality of the bodybuilder is as much on display as physical development.

Lisa won that contest with a graceful and attractive posing routine. It was not, however, one I would have wanted to employ. But looking back, I can see I didn't grasp that the strength of Lisa's routine was that she was using it as a means of personal expression. Of course her routine wasn't right for me; it wasn't supposed to be.

In my next contest, I presented myself in the same way I had before, and this time I didn't even place. What upset me so much is that I knew I was among the best two or three in that event, and I couldn't understand why the judges had failed to recognize this.

Actually, we had all failed to some extent. I had not learned to show off my physique to its best advantage, and the judges were unable to overlook this inexperience and judge my physique on its own merits. But I had to accept the fact that, right or wrong, it's the judges who pick the winners, and I had better learn to present myself in such a way as to get their votes and yet not compromise my own standards.

"Don't let yourself turn into a martyr," Bill Dobbins told me after the contest. "It's no use being ahead of the times and helping to educate the audience and the judges if all you do is take a lot of lumps and don't get anything out of it yourself."

The way things were going, nobody was more aware of the truth of this than I was. So I had to rethink what I was doing. I made a virtue of necessity. I realized I would never be able to win a contest without an exciting, polished posing routine. I began to refine my routine as I learned more about myself and my relationship with the audience. Previously, I had thought of posing as a series of static positions, but now I began to consider the transitions between the poses. As I did more analyzing, I came to see that many poses used by men are designed primarily to display mass, and they simply don't work for a woman, no matter how much muscularity and definition she may have.

Mass is nonetheless a factor in bodybuilding for women as well as men, because simply shaping muscles means, to some degree, filling

them out with the right kind of mass. But there is so much more to look for in a championship physique: muscle tone, density, proportion, symmetry, and personal qualities like grace, confidence and charisma. No, as important as flexing your muscles may be to your routine, there's a lot more to posing than just jumping up on a platform and hitting some muscle shots.

Initially my feelings were hurt by the well-meaning criticism leveled at me by my friends. But then I began to invite it. I listened carefully to the diverse opinions of Joe Weider, Lisa Lyon, Stacey Bentley, Bill Dobbins and others, and I began to take notes and really think about what

Every competitive posing routine should include several back poses, such as this graceful stance.

they said. I consulted makeup artists, hair stylists, actors and anyone else whose advice might be helpful in improving my presentation onstage.

All that work paid off. Although I trained very hard for this year's contests, I believe it was the improvement in my presentation, and not my physique, that gave me the victory in the California Women's Bodybuilding Championship. Bodybuilding, I have come to accept, is more than just a difficult athletic undertaking—it's a dramatic art as well.

The first thing I did in creating my new routine was to limit myself to a few basic moves. Better to do a few poses well than a lot of them badly, I figured. And then I practiced, at least an hour a day. This not only increased my fluency in these movements, but I found it was a terrific exercise as well.

In addition to the poses, there are the transitions between them. Some men tend to overlook this part of the presentation, but there's no reason for any women to make the same mistake. After all, grace and beauty of movement are considered feminine attributes, so why not cash in on them?

Then I discovered the importance of music to a posing routine. I had always thought the music was just there for background, or to entertain the audience. Now I realized that the rhythm of the music and the emotions it engendered helped to create a more expressive and dramatic posing routine. Music is one more element in the artistic whole.

But I never forgot that I was a bodybuilder, not a dancer or a gymnast. Grace of movement and imagination in presentation are well and good, but a bodybuilder is up there to display the body. Therefore, at some point, you simply have to stop and pose. And you have to hold that pose long enough for the judges to make an evaluation of the development of your physique.

After a while the most effective poses for me began to evolve. I studied myself in the mirror and spent countless hours looking at photographs, films and video tapes of my posing routine. I gradually found myself abandoning the masculine poses I had done at the beginning and substituting more feminine versions to display the same body parts. But I didn't do this because of some preconception of what kind of presentation was natural to the male or the female. It was strictly a pragmatic, trial-and-error process in which I used what worked and threw out what didn't.

No more clenched-fist, double-biceps shots.

No lat spreads, or Most Muscular poses. I found other ways of showing off my arms, back, chest, etc. I felt I had a better physique than most of my competitors, and I wanted the judges to realize it.

My greatest insight was the realization that my posing should be an expression of myself, my own personality and identity. And now the selection process took on a new meaning. My posing routines were no longer assembled in a mechanical fashion, but grew out of my innermost desires and feelings. Posing is a form of communication. You use it to tell the audience who you are. After all, most of the people don't know you, and so you use this nonverbal means to introduce yourself. I had seen Lisa do it, and then Stacey—and finally I learned how to do it myself.

I learned to relate to the audience at all times. I had seen that they have no interest in competitors so self-absorbed that they forget a transaction is taking place. The audience responds to indifference with indifference.

During this period of my development, I was often unaware of what was taking place. A lot of it was unconscious. However, since I have had time to look back and reflect, I'm in a better position to answer the questions I get so often from women bodybuilders who want to know how to pose. I tell them:

1. Watch other women contestants, learn from them, but don't imitate them slavishly. A pose that's right for others is not necessarily right for you.
2. Practice, then practice some more. An hour a day is not too much.
3. Keep your routine short and simple. Most events limit you to a minute onstage, and I usually go shorter than that. Show off your good points, hold the pose long enough for the judges to get a good look, but don't wear out your welcome.
4. Learn from your mistakes. Admitting you've made some can hurt your pride, but it gets you further in the long run.
5. Ask yourself why you're doing each pose. What are you trying to achieve? Is it going to do what you expect it to?
6. Don't forget the other aspects of presentation—hair style, makeup, posing costume, whatever. Everything that affects your appearance onstage plays a part in winning or losing.

Some questions don't have simple answers. You learn a little at a time. For instance, I did a photo session for Joe Weider a while ago and in the process he gave me some valuable suggestions on how to pose and what sort of costume would be best.

Every time something like this hapens, I try to take advantage of it. The art of presentation is developed much like a bodybuilder's physique—step by step.

Women have a great opportunity in bodybuilding. We aren't tied down to traditions created by generations before us, and we aren't limited to copying the men. In fact, if we use our creative imaginations and really explore all the possibilities, they'll end up learning from us.

But we mustn't forget that we are bodybuilders. The name of the game is still

Women's poses should emphasize both grace of presentation and complete physical development.

exercise and diet for maximum muscular development, symmetry and display. Along with grace, we've got to include strength. This is not a beauty contest, however much aesthetic appeal is involved.

Sexiness used blatantly is inappropriate for bodybuilding competitions. So are coy little "feminine" moves onstage. Some judges right now may actually fall for that cute stuff but they're on their way out.

After all the months devoted to preparation, that moment when you pose in front of a live audience is a thrilling experience. For your own sake and the audience's, come to the stage thoroughly prepared. Learn from your mistakes—and successes. When you step off the stage, be certain that you did all you could to present an exciting, professional performance.

Food for Women in Training

by Mandy Tanny

In the strenuous world of women's bodybuilding, going on the normal type of diet is hardly ever productive in the long term. But if you reeducate your tastebuds to like foods that are good for you, half the battle is won.

When you're working out hard, your finely tuned body will tell you what it needs. By eating a healthful, balanced diet, you won't have uncontrollable food cravings, and you'll be too proud of your physical improvement to eat junk foods.

When you're grinding out regular workouts, you must think less about body weight and more about the fitness level of your muscle. Forget about the number of calories you're burning. As for diet, it won't work without exercise. Exercise tones and increases the amount of muscle, changes its chemistry and increases its metabolic rate. Also, muscle that's in condition uses more calories, both at work and at rest.

Your body needs fat to function properly. Fat mainly provides muscles with fuel. Normally, even when you're not exercising, the energy needs of your muscle are met by both fat and glucose. Much of the fat in the food you eat is burned off daily. If you ate 60 grams (2 ounces) of fat a day, your normal metabolism would burn it off.

It's easy to run out of glucose when you train, but you are unlikely ever to run out of fat. Fat is an efficient, compactly stored source of energy, and it looks bad only when there's too much of it. That is why it's so difficult for a beginner to lose weight through exercise alone. A pound of fat has 3500 calories. Theoretically, in the course of a 26-mile race, a marathon runner receives only 1200 calories from fat stores, with an additional 1200 supplied by glycogen. So she burns about *one-third* of a pound of fat.

Since you burn a great deal of glucose during bodybuilding exercises, your blood sugar drops, which stirs your appetite for carbohydrate. If you aren't careful, and you eat spaghetti or white bread instead of complex carbohydrate like fresh vegetables, whose natural fiber cuts down absorption of calories in the small intestine, you run the risk of an insulin overload reaction that drives your blood sugar abnormally high. This high blood sugar cannot be processed fast enough by the muscle cells, so it goes to the fat cells, where it's readily admitted and turned into triglycerides (fat).

This peculiar problem can escalate particularly in beginning bodybuilders. If you are fat and you start out by training too hard, you resist burning the fat you're trying to lose. You also get fatter

Omelettes are an appetizing way to meet daily protein requirements.

by eating the wrong carbohydrates you crave.

If you block that reaction by wrongly refusing to eat any carbohydrate after exercise, you don't lessen the blood sugar problem. The liver begins to take over, converting available protein (muscle) into glucose for energy. There goes your hard-won muscle tissue, and those desired curves to boot. In addition, with the loss of muscle tissue, you lose the ability to do the work necessary to burn off fat. Like a silly pup, you find yourself chasing your tail.

The female hormonal system is more complex than the male system. Along with the fact that women have 30% less muscle cell mass and 20% more fat cells, their weight-gain problem is greater. Reduction of calories alone doesn't always solve the problem. In fact, cutting down on foods consumed may lead to deficiencies. In a Johns Hopkins School of Medicine study on overweight people (hundreds of subjects, mostly women, were used) it was found that a large majority were deficient in many vitamins, minerals and amino acids. In addition, almost all these subjects, especially the women, were not producing enough of the adreno-cortico steroid hormones. When these hormones were brought back into normal production with the addition of certain oils in the diet, many vital metabolic functions also returned to normal.

Most people attempting to diet away fat assume right off that they should reduce their fat intake because fat has double the calories of either carbohydrate or protein. But clinical studies indicate that fats alone do not cause fatty deposits in the body. In fact, small amounts of animal fats from meat, fish oils, eggs and cream, along with linoleic acid derived from vegetable oils, are vital to normal metabolism.

Carbohydrate is essential to the utilization of fat. Carbohydrate (glucose) can be compared to kindling wood. It provides a quick flame and high heat and helps ignite the big log (fat) in the fireplace. The enzymes in muscle that burn glucose differ from the enzymes that burn fat. If you haven't been exercising, the fat-burning enzymes are weak. So the more out of shape and the fatter you are, the less able you are to burn fat. When you're not in shape, your blood uses glucose and resists using fat for energy. In other words, the more fat you have stored, the less fat you'll burn.

When planning your daily menu, include an adequate amount of protein (at least 20 grams at each meal), consisting of meat, fish, poultry, cheese or eggs. Four ounces of meat, fish or poultry equals 25 grams; one egg is 6 grams; one ounce of cheese is 7 grams; one cup of cottage cheese is 20 grams. Four small meals a day should provide a total of 80 grams of protein. A milk-and-egg protein supplement mixed in

Dairy products and seafood are other good sources of high quality protein in a woman's daily diet.

nonfat milk makes a satisfactory meal replacement.

Johns Hopkins and Columbia University studies have confirmed that milk and egg protein has the highest biological value. Animal protein provides all the essential amino acids in amounts necessary to maintain cells.

Avoid refined or processed carbohydrates. Use only raw fruits and vegetables for your sugar. For losing weight, keep your carbohydrates at about 40–50 grams daily. Keep it at 80 grams to maintain weight. If you're working out hard, you may need even more. But if your carbs come from raw, natural sources, your appetite will be your guide.

Use polyunsaturated oil dressing for salads. Butter is better than margarine, which is partially hardened and does not supply a good ratio of the essential fatty acids.

Don't forget the "specific dynamic action" of foods. All foods require a certain amount of energy to digest, some more than others. Most protein foods and all leafy green and fibrous green vegetables require up to 33% more energy to digest than they provide. The necessary calories are drawn from your fat stores, and the result is a body weight loss when you eat such foods as lettuce, cucumbers, asparagus or green beans.

When you lack a single vitamin or mineral, the

The body of Shelley Gruwell, World Grand Prix Bodybuilding Champion, is largely a product of careful attention to diet.

chemistry of all body cells is thrown off balance. The function of hormones, the production of enzymes, and the biosynthesis of nucleic acids and proteins are all impaired. The foods we eat don't necessarily supply all these vital elements. A vitamin/mineral supplement should contain the fullest complement of lipotropic elements along with the vital minerals.

Remember, nobody advertises unprocessed food. When processors spend money to tamper with food, they have to get their money back. The fiber in unrefined carbohydrates like raw vegetables gives you a feeling of fullness and prevents you from eating too much. It soaks up water in your stomach and tends to satisfy your hunger.

The way to survive in this carbohydrate environment is to eliminate refined sugars and flours and any food that contains corn syrup, sucrose, dextrose, lactose, corn sugar and other aliases for refined sugar. If you eat in restaurants, stick with the plainest, most natural food items you can find on the menu. Ask a lot of questions as you order.

Training success depends on maximum nutrition and total cell nourishment. Eat several small meals daily, making sure that each meal includes protein. Eat a salad every day. Eat whole fruit; avoid squeezed juices. Take multiple vitamins and minerals. Keep carbohydrates low. Keep fats low, but balanced between saturated (animal fats) and unsaturated (vegetable) fats. The proper nutrition will take you a long way toward that body you want.

Updating Your Anti-Fat Diet

by Mandy Tanny

The tyranny of diets continues to oppress the overweight. Diets, per se, don't work. Nor can you successfully control your body weight with regular exercise (if you eat too much), or sensible nutrition (if you eat too much), or behavior modification (if all you think about is food).

A great portion of the American consciousness is occupied with losing weight. Weight-loss groups like The Diet Workshop, Overeaters Anonymous and Weight Watchers can boast only marginal success.

Those terrific fad diets guaranteed to make you splendidly thin, like the Nine-Day Wonder Diet, The Scarsdale Diet, The Crash-Off-Ten-Pounds-in-One-Week Diet, ad infinitum, usually set time limits because your body may possibly resort to using its own protein for energy resulting in a loss of good solid muscle tissue instead of fat. You lose weight all right, but you aren't going to look slinky.

Body weight is the whipping-boy of diet plans. The real culprit is fat. Everybody knows how to get rid of body weight, but despite eviction notices, fat always seems to remain the star boarder. Recent studies that combine experience with biochemical and nutritional analyses which disclose the active changes in metabolism offer the most logical way out of the maze.

Mandy Tanny has more than ten years of experience in the health club business. She's helped over 100,000 women to improve their health, fitness, and appearance through weight training.

If your car isn't running well, don't drive around looking for a better gasoline—better you should have it tuned up. In the same way, you should change your thinking from body weight to the *fitness level* of your muscle. Forget the ideal body weight and the number of calories you are burning. Don't addle your brain.

Outside of a few simple diet rules which you likely already know, your main concern is the

41

function of enzymes in your muscle and the effect exercise has on them. Ignore body weight, and let girth measurements be your guide. Along with a mirror they will better indicate the condition you are in.

The answer then is *exercise* and sensible, *nutritious food*—not too little and not too much of either. As you progress, the pride in your accomplishment provides a powerful stimulus. As your dress size shrinks, you gain control, and that means power. No one likes to give up power.

The fatter you are, the more your body has adapted to a low-calorie intake. It takes little excess food to make you even fatter. "But I eat less than most people," you lament. Which is true. Therefore, it must be something in your body chemistry favoring the deposit of fat.

There are two types of fat: the kind you can see and pinch and the hidden intramuscular fat. It also seems that the subcutaneous fat burns off before the intramuscular fat. That's why you can't tell how lean you are by the simple pinch test. The underwater weighing method more accurately determines your Lean Body Mass. Women normally have about 22% body fat, but the average is closer to 36% in America.

You start to gain weight when you have eaten too much and exercised too little. At first, fat replaces unused muscle, becoming intramuscular. You won't notice a gain in body weight in the beginning because of the exchange. As time goes by and more fat is deposited, it begins to creep outside the muscles and settle under the skin. The body weight starts to go up.

If you hadn't exercised, chances are you would not sink if you took the body weight tank test. You wouldn't have enough dense muscle to sink you. By the time you have become fat and overweight, you are badly out of shape. It may take five years for the sedentary life to make you fat if you had been active and thin all your life before that. It comes as a shock when that happens, and the task of getting rid of that fat is not so simple. The wonderful diets you read about would make you think so, however.

The fact that you are carrying excess fat isn't so bad. It is the out-of-shape muscle trying to support that fat that's your problem. There are a lot of great male athletes—football players, wrestlers, weightlifters and field-track men—who are way overweight, yet enjoy robust, good health, and they move with extreme agility. Few women fall in this category, but if you look close you'll notice some rather hefty ones among star tennis players and certainly golfers. The average fat woman doesn't have the athlete's luck.

As for diet, it won't work without exercise. Exercise tones, increases the amount of muscle, changes its chemistry and ups its metabolic rate. Best of all, in-shape muscle utilizes more calories when you are at rest or asleep.

Don't get the idea that if moderate exercise is good, strenuous exercise is better. I see some women get swept away with their diet and training programs. Elated with the realization they are beginning to lose weight, they step up their training—more days at the gym, increased jogging miles—and adhere rigidly to their diets. They get an 'A' for effort, but generally when they do that, they don't see what I see: they have lost a lot of muscle tissue and look haggard.

I know right away what they are doing, because I did the same thing for a brief period until I caught on and bridled my enthusiasm. I still have to be careful to eat enough basic carbohydrate, fruit, vegetables, nuts or grains, when I am trying to "rip-up" for a photo session so that my energy demand isn't tapping into muscle protein which diminishes the hard-won muscle size and shape.

I run to complement my bodybuilding. They are a good combination, but I have to be careful not to overtrain. In the excitement of training you can consume more energy than you replace. That is particularly hard on your bodybuilding, because you don't have the energy to do the exercise with enough force and intensity to build shape and size. Over a period of a few years. I have combined the two successfully. At the present time my pulse will drop to 100 within seconds after I finish a three-mile run. During the run it varies between 120 and 150.

I run because of the proven fat-burning aerobic effect and because I like it. To effectively burn fat, however, you have to run for at least 12 minutes. I run about 30 minutes as a warmup before each bodybuilding session.

Regardless of the exercise you do, exercise must be part of your diet. That is why I stress it over telling you what and how to eat. It doesn't matter what kind of exercise you do, as long as you do it long enough to be effective. Fifteen minutes of running is comparable to two hours of tennis. Studies seem to show that moderate exercise over extended periods of time is best for fat metabolism.

If you walk four hours a day, you can do yourself as much good as running for 30 minutes or bodybuilding for an hour. A four-hour walk doesn't mean that you will build bodybuilding-type muscle or develop a high oxygen uptake, but you will change the muscle chemistry and strengthen the fat-burning enzymes in muscle tissue that are ordinarily so fragile.

The enzymes in muscle that burn glucose are different from the enzymes that burn fat. The more out of shape and fat you are, the weaker your fat-burning muscle enzymes are, so the glucose-burning enzymes take over. Therefore, blood glucose is used, and the fat is ignored.

So the more fat you have, the less fat you burn. If you try to offset that condition by eating less carbohydrate, the liver then converts protein into glucose, and you lose valuable muscle tissue. This in turn causes a loss of the fat-burning enzymes, and you are caught in a diabolical circle.

Enzymes used in fat breakdown need a lot of oxygen. That is one of the reasons I include running in my training. Running is aerobic, but bodybuilding, as women presently practice it, is largely anerobic. That means bodybuilding burns less fat than running. Yet, competition male bodybuilders take long weight workouts—without resorting to running—that are obviously fat burners. I think I could get along without the running and stay trim with solid muscle, but I would have to train a bit faster and longer in the gym and be particularly careful of my fat intake.

Before you start dieting you should start exercising. Better yet, do them both. Just remember that exercise, any kind, strengthens the enzymes in the muscle that burn fat.

With that load off my chest, I feel I can tell you more honestly how the diet that has worked for me can also work for you. Dieting is half of your training. You won't look fantastic unless you remove the fat that is covering the muscle.

Let me say at the outset, you have to stay hungry. Stay away from a variety of foods. Limit yourself to a dozen basic food items. Stay away from all dairy products except for a spoonful of yogurt every few days for the bacterial benefit in the intestines.

Eat raw vegetables only. Or if you must, steam them lightly, but raw roughage is best for moving food along in the intestine and regulating the absorption of calories. Stay away from sugar and honey. Don't use salt or other condiments. Drink a lot of water.

Multiple small meals may satisfy you and keep you from gaining weight. But if you are really serious, it is best to eat two small meals a day. If

the food is basic and pure, you won't need much food at all.

I will drink a glass of fresh juice for breakfast. My lunch consists of a piece of fruit and a hard-boiled egg. Dinner is a raw salad with fish or chicken or one of the glandular meats, plus a piece of fruit.

You should have your carbohydrate in the morning, juice or whatever. You don't need protein because you haven't done anything to require it. Remember, protein only lasts for two hours in your system. It is best to eat it after you work out when it's vital for growth and repair.

I eat a lot of eggs. I may also eat them in place of fish or meat for dinner. Take vitamin supplements with your juice in the morning.

If I really feel a need for it, I will eat a hard-boiled egg or more rarely a piece of cheese, an hour before I work out. Eat a piece of whole grain bread or a dish of whole grain cereal occasionally. They have a high fiber content, but you won't need them often when you are

Mandy favors Seated Alternate Dumbbell Curls to tone the muscles of her arms.

getting enough fresh fruits and vegetables. Grains tend to bloat you up and bog you down for your workouts. They are fairly high in carbohydrate. Eat grain twice a week to be on the safe side.

My salad dressing consists of a couple of tablespoons full of cold-pressed vegetable oil with vinegar, stretched out with fresh lemon juice. Do use it sparingly, however.

Coffee has become one of the secrets of the trade. It curbs the appetite. Taken just before a workout, it helps metabolize fat, but four cups a day should be the maximum.

Don't eat after 6 p.m. Your functions slow down at night when you are generally at rest, and you burn fewer calories.

Raw nuts and raw seeds are excellent snack foods. They are a good source of protein, carbohydrate and roughage. They are very satisfying. Avoid diet sodas. Why perpetuate the craving for sweets?

If you must eat in restaurants, carefully scrape off whatever the food is cooked in. Don't touch anything fried.

I keep this little formula in my head: If you leave the table feeling full, you are going to gain. If you leave the table feeling satisfied, you will maintain. If you leave the table feeling hungry, you will lose.

Eat organ meats preferably: liver, heart, kidney, sweetbreads or brains. Limit servings of red meat to once a week. At best it is high in fat. Stay away from anything artificial like margarine. If you must, eat butter. If you are really serious about staying in shape with training, avoid potatoes. They are cooked, which means they are processed, and the nutrients you get won't be worth the extra calories.

Bodybuilders who strive for that lean look must stay hungry. Metaphorically it means they must crave success. That's a pretty good bodybuilding motto.

Stay hungry!

And train hard!

Training and Menstrual Function

by Mandy Tanny

It's a known fact, although somewhat suppressed, that women who participate in strenuous activities are generally subject to menstrual irregularities. Heretofore, not a great deal has been said about it because the women themselves, particularly those in the limelight, hesitate to discuss it for fear they might lose some of the sports equality that they are so grimly clutching.

Two researchers, Leon Speroff, M.D., and David Redwine, M.D., both of the Department of Obstetrics and Gynecology at the University of Oregon Health Sciences Center, published a questionnaire in a Portland newspaper the day after a big marathon. They wanted to obtain objective information about the relationship of running to menstrual function, body weight and weight loss. They received nearly 900 answers.

Publishing the questionnaire in a newspaper opened a can of worms because the editors headlined it: "Is Jogging Harmful to a Woman's Health?" Such a question was not the intent of the researchers, who mainly were concerned with detecting trends and new directions for further investigation. Many women thought the headline was misleading, damaging and sensational, that it reinforced sexist myths,

created false fears, and was irresponsible and absurd. Many others emphasized the positive contributions that exercise made to their lives. Indeed, the emotion that the headline stirred up clearly showed the need to accumulate reliable data on the subject.

Although the study was specifically directed to running, the findings could well be reinforced by looking at other strenuous sports activities. There has not yet been a controlled study on women bodybuilders, but the anecdotal accounts by women in weight training tend to support the present accumulated data on menstrual trends in runners.

Data on age, height, weight, weight loss, duration and speed of running, menstrual function and pregnancy were solicited by the questionnaire. Although there's no significance to the statistics associated with pregnancy, it is interesting to note that of the total number of respondents, 7.3% were pregnant and running; 3.3% were breast-feeding and running; and 14.2% had run during a pregnancy. Forty-seven percent had never been pregnant, and only 18.3% of the 115 women who had aborted or had a premature delivery did so during the period when they were running. (A case that

Sit-ups done on a slantboard firm the stomach muscles. Simply hook your feet under the board's restraints and do your sit-ups.

even as we look forward to it. Rationalize no longer, because *Muscle & Fitness* has a shape-up plan designed exclusively for you!

YOU ARE HOW YOU BEHAVE

Bad habits lead to lowered energy levels, less attractive bodies and a depressed mental outlook. Good habits can alleviate many of these symptoms. There are three basic areas that you have to consider when planning to get yourself in shape for summer—

- How you eat
- How you exercise
- How you take care of your body

Weight control and overall conditioning come about through a combination of diet and exercise—one without the other is just not very effective. Attention to personal hygiene gives us a psychological lift and often reflects how others treat us. Healthy, happy people seem to cope better and have more fun.

BEHAVIOR MODIFICATION

Before you start your summer shape-up plan, keep in mind that permanent change comes slowly. Habits should be altered a little at a time—you can't change overnight from being sedentary to highly athletic. Nor can you go from being an overweight type to being chic-slim in one easy lesson. Habits are the patterns of behavior to which we have become

accustomed. It takes a while to adapt to a new form of behavior. But the benefits, however small, begin immediately—and you'll feel satisfied and more confident every day.

EATING AND EXERCISE: THE VITAL BALANCE

Mass obesity is a relatively modern disease. In other cultures, other times, our ancestors had to work too hard and got too little to eat to worry much about putting on too much weight. Never before in history have people found high-caloric food so readily available nor lived a lifestyle so unconducive to exercise.

The results? The average American male has a relative body fat content of 15%. For women, the figure is 25%. And that's the average. That means half the population is even fatter than that.

It has been said that "you are what you eat." Taking that statement a step farther, we can say, "you are what you do." Eating is behavior. It is a learned activity—a habit. So is the type and amount of exercise you get. Together, these two things are the most significant determinants of your body's appearance. Unused muscle gets atrophied, flabby and loses shape. A body coated with excess fat loses all definition. The first step in your summer shape-up program is to find out how your eating and exercise behavior can be modified to produce the kind of body that is your heart's desire—one that looks good because it is healthy. The two go together.

EATING: THERE'S NO MYSTERY ABOUT IT

The word "diet" is commonly misused. It should merely refer to the way in which you eat, rather than a special program of eating for weight loss. The fact is, most diets don't work. The diet industry pulls in about 10 billion dollars a year, but only 12 out of every 100 dieters actually manage to lose a significant amount of weight, and only two of those refrain from putting the weight back on. That is not a very impressive record.

Whenever you take in more energy in the form of calories than your body can use, it stores the excess as fat. That means simply that being overweight comes from overeating. The tiny fraction of people who are overweight because of metabolic problems are hardly worth mentioning. Bodybuilders learned the secret a long time ago: to lose weight, eat less. Nothing else is necessary, given a fixed level of caloric expenditure through exercise.

Leg Raises can also be done on a slantboard. The higher you raise the head end of the board, the more intensely this exercise stresses your stomach muscles.

Eating is habit. It is a form of behavior that can be modified. And it must be permanently modified if you are to lose weight and continue to keep it off. Fad diets won't do any good because, after you abandon them, you tend to revert back to your old eating habits and regain the same weight. What you need to do is learn a few basic principles about how and what to eat in order to lose weight and keep it off. Incorporate these new behaviors into your routine a little at a time, as quickly as comfort will allow. The result will be a better looking, better feeling you—for summer and a lifetime of fun.

CALORIES AND NUTRITION

Too many diets attempt to restrict your intake of calories while ignoring the body's basic nutritional needs. The "basic food groups"—the grains, meats, fruits and vegetables, dairy products—provide the body with protein, carbohydrate, fats, vitamins and minerals.

Balanced nutrition demands that the body receive each of these elements, but it doesn't need all of them all the time. Certainly, it helps if you have a little protein at each meal instead of a lot all at once, but the body has a way of compensating for imbalances in the short term. It's when a deprivation continues over a long period that you begin to get into trouble. Unfortunately, that's exactly what most diets set out to accomplish.

Weight loss tends to come slowly—two or three pounds a week at the most. It is a fact that

when the body metabolizes a pound of fat, roughly a pound of water is created in the process. This means that actual weight loss is not immediately noticeable. It takes time for this excess water to cycle out of the system, so if you go on a diet that seems to result in 8 or 10 pounds of weight loss the first week, you are probably measuring the effects of dehydration— a common effect of low-carbohydrate diets like those of Drs. Stillman and Atkins. That weight loss is meaningless in the long run.

To lose weight, you want to burn fat—*not* muscle tissue. A balanced diet causes you to burn fat; otherwise, you are causing the body to extract energy from muscle tissue, and this is obviously undesirable. A good, basic standard of nutritional balance endorsed by the government is:

- Fat: 30%
  Saturated fats, 10%
  Unsaturated fats, 20%
- Protein: 12%
- Carbohydrates: 58%
  Complex carbs, 43%
  Sugar, 15%

PLANNING YOUR SUMMER MEALS

There are lots of diets around that will tell you what to leave out. Sugar, for one—everybody knows that sugar is all calories and no nutrition. Honey, some don't know, is just as bad. There are plenty of guides around to tell you what the caloric, protein, carbohydrate and fat content of various foods may be. But how do you make all of this palatable? If you don't enjoy a particular way of eating, you sure aren't going to follow it for long. Here are a few hints:

1. Rediscover the salad.
2. Re-examine "fattening" food.
3. Eat less meat.
4. Cut back on all fats.
5. Add fruit rather than sugar to cereals.
6. Keep whole grains on your menu.
7. Go heavy on the vegetables.
8. Use common sense.
9. Enjoy what you eat.

KEEPING SCORE

The best way to keep track of caloric intake and nutritional balance is to keep a food diary. That's what many bodybuilders do and it works, but unless you are terribly motivated, it gets to holding a dumbbell in your hand. I use a simple concrete brick that's about four inches high. I do two sets of 25 reps on each leg. Some days I will use the bent-leg style, lowering the heel all the way down and coming up slow all the way. On other days I will put the accent on the upward motion, bouncing up as high and fast as possible, with the legs locked straight. By doing Calf Raises one leg at a time, the work becomes concentrated and the calves really develop. You won't miss the calf machine at all.

The barbell, that all-purpose free weight, is ideal for doing Deadlifts, Rowing motions or the Good Morning exercise. I do four sets of 12 reps on the Deadlift one day, and four sets of 12 reps on the Good Morning exercise the next day, alternating between the two lifts. Every time I train I will also do Bent-Over Rows—three sets of 12 reps.

Back Raises can be done off the edge of the flat bench with the feet held down by a towel or strap tied around the bench. Although you only lower the upper body about halfway before the head touches the floor, there is still a sufficient range of movement upward to make the lower back muscles fully contract. I get the fullest effect with a single set of 30 reps.

Training the triceps is an area of major concern at the health spas. Triceps exercises are included in every program, and spas have a lot of machines and pulleys to do the job. I do a simple movement at home called the Triceps Kickback, a specialty of the top musclemen. Bend forward holding a dumbbell in one hand, upper arm pressed close to the body and parallel to the floor, with the forearm down. Extend the forearm back to a straight-arm position, and return, always maintaining the horizontal position of the upper arm. I like to do a couple of sets of 12 reps with each arm. This one really tightens and shapes the triceps.

To develop the deltoids, I do three sets (12 reps per set) of Lateral Raises with dumbbells. I follow these with three sets of alternate Front Dumbbell Raises, 12 reps per set. I also get a lot of front deltoid work from Flat and Incline Presses (again, three sets—12 reps). You can do them either with dumbbells or the barbell.

For the more advanced woman bodybuilder, the chinning bar is a worthwhile addition. Chins are not as difficult as you think. You may not be able to do one the first time, but within a few months you could be doing a dozen of them. Just keep trying. They are an excellent exercise for upper back development. The portable doorway chin bar is easy to install. It can also be used for stretching between sets—by simply hanging from it.

There are several ways of working the abdominals, of course. You can do Leg Raises hanging from the chin bar or reclining against a slant board placed against a wall. Both flatten the lower midsection. You can also do Crunches, the exercise where you lie on the floor with your heels resting on a bench, knees bent, contracting the abdominals by raising the shoulders a few inches off the floor. I get the best effect from any abdominal exercise if I do around 30 reps.

The evening is a good time for a home gym workout. It's quiet; the workday is over. You can work to exhaustion and go right to bed. It does you more good than television. It keeps you out of the refrigerator.

You can warm up with a five- or ten-minute jog around the block, or you can skip rope. Also, make sure you have extra weights to keep pace with your growing strength.

What I like about working out at home is that you can set your own pace, play your own type of music, there are no distractions, you can try new ways of doing exercises without having to explain to idle onlookers, and you can grunt and groan and huff and puff to your heart's content. A curious neghbor will soon become a training partner. Or better yet, it's easy to get your husband or boyfriend to be your training partner. There's no better activity two people can share.

Shaping Up at Any Age

by Betty Weider

Fitness is a lifetime concern—or at least it should be. After all, life itself is a form of athletic event, and we are only issued one body with which to get through it. Age does exact its toll in the long run, but this doesn't mean we should take that sitting down, literally. Proper exercise and nutrition is the way to fight back.

Actually, most of us have the wrong idea about the effects of age on our bodies. Much of what we regard as signs of aging are just the effects of neglect and deterioration. When you look at men and women who have really worked at physical fitness all their lives, it's often virtually impossible to tell their ages.

But the body changes with time, and so do its needs. A teenager is very different physically from a 40-year-old. Therefore, staying physically fit all your life means that you have to take these physical changes into consideration.

Surprisingly, the kind of exercise and diet that you need at different ages is pretty much the same. What changes is just the emphasis, the priorities you have to observe. You use the same sort of recipe; you just alter the proportion of the ingredients.

The hardest part of any program is simply getting started. The young procrastinate, thinking they have all the time in the world. Older people are reluctant, believing that they're already too late. Neither of these attitudes is correct.

The younger you are, the more results you're going to get from exercise and good nutrition. But the older you are, the more important physical fitness becomes in combating the gradual loss of physical powers that comes with age.

So whether you're 14, 24, 44, or more, it's time to shape up for health, strength, beauty and fitness. And as for getting started, there's no time like the present!

TEEN FITNESS

When a young man reaches puberty, his body is flooded with testosterone. A lot of boys become skinny teenagers who never gain a pound no matter what they eat.

With women, it's just the opposite. Puberty brings on increased estrogen levels, and many teenage girls have a constant battle on their hands to keep from getting chubby. This stage passes, but not nearly fast enough to suit most girls. And the danger exists that poor exercise

55

and nutritional habits learned at this age can result in poor fitness and health down the line.

But women approaching their 20th year, as is the case with men, are nearly at the height of their physical powers. They can achieve a higher heart rate and are capable of great physical endurance. Because the body is so responsive to training at this age, you can lay down a foundation of fitness that will serve you well the rest of your life.

THE 20S

A teenage girl may be active in various sports in school—e.g., softball, basketball, volleyball, swimming and track. But a woman in her 20s has to go out of her way to find opportunities for exerting herself physically. Social pressures still make mature women more sedentary than men.

A woman is at her strongest in her 20s, and so she benefits the most from resistance-type exercises. However, as the age of 30 approaches, the body begins to slow down. The metabolism changes, and a real weight problem can develop if the diet is not altered appropriately.

It has been estimated that your caloric need diminishes 5% between 20 and 35, and 2–3% per decade after that until age 60. Another way of looking at this is that your caloric need diminishes by about 10 calories per day per year after ages 25–30—which means you may well put on one pound a year, or 10 pounds in 10 years, unless you modify your eating and exercise habits.

THE 30S

In your 30s, you start leaving your youth behind. Oh, you may still be young at 35, but you're not youthful. The body has matured and, if you haven't taken steps to keep it fit, it may be showing signs of wear and tear.

Many women at this age are mothers, and their bodies may show indications of having given birth. This is the age when weight may become a serious problem and physical difficulties such as lower back pain can manifest themselves.

But old age does not begin at 30. You can keep your weight down by controlling your calorie balance. You can keep your youthful appearance through good nutrition and well-rounded exercise programs. Proper nutrition and exercise also prevent such things as back problems and even the development of age-related disease, such as cardiac trouble.

THE 40S

Women have feared the 40s unnecessarily. True, the metabolism does slow down even more at this age, which makes it easier to gain weight. And most housewives and mothers, as well as hard-working career women, do not get much encouragement to devote themselves to physical training. Also, women of this age may require calcium supplementation to keep their bones strong and healthy.

But these are minor inconveniences, easily overcome. Women bodybuilders such as Florida's Doris Barrilleaux, who has just turned 49, are still capable of standing onstage next to girls of 20 and blowing them away in competition. It's all a matter of whether or not you take the time and trouble to eat right and get enough exercise.

Menopause is a time when many women experience both mental and physical difficulties. But the fact is, the better the shape you're in, the healthier and more physically confident you become, and the less you have to fear from natural biological changes in your own body.

THE 50S AND BEYOND

After you reach 50, neglect of the body can result in nonreversible aging. When you are younger, diet and exercise can actually reverse the aging process to some degree. But not so after 50. Therefore, taking care of yourself at this age becomes of utmost importance.

Yet, in some ways, it gets a lot easier. Athletes have long known that it's easier to maintain physical development and condition than it is to create it in the first place. It's amazing what effect even gentle exercise can have on a person aged 50 or 60. The right kind of program can enable the body to maintain virtually its full capacities to incredibly advanced ages. Witness the elderly farmers and workmen who are still out lifting, hauling and laboring in their 90s and beyond. "Use it or lose it" is the old saying, and it's still very true.

FITNESS FOR ANY AGE

There are three basic needs that any complete physical fitness program must provide:

1. *Cardiovascular conditioning*— The heart and circulatory system.
2. *Muscular Conditioning*—The strength and

firmness of the body's skeletal muscles.
3. *Flexibility*—The achievement of full range of motion of all the joints and extremities.

These three components of fitness remain important all your life, but they're required in different proportions as you grow older (see below:)

Teens

1. Lots of sports and general conditioning.
2. Begin to build body structure through resistance training.
3. Maintain youthful flexibility.

20s

1. Make an effort to stay active.
2. Maintain cardiovascular conditioning.
3. Make a greater effort to build strength and muscle firmness through resistance training.
4. Balance off weight training with additional stretching.

30s

1. Add more abdominal training to your fitness program.
2. Continue to keep the heart and skeletal muscles in good condition. Also, work on stretching to counteract the shrinking effect caused by gravity acting on the body.

40s

1. Avoid tendency to slack off on training at this age.
2. Maintain resistance training and slightly increase cardiovascular training to offset lower metabolic rate.

50s and Beyond

1. Maintain cardiovascular training.
2. Emphasize flexibility and stretching.
3. Incorporate moderate resistance training.

PHYSICAL ACTIVITY

There is no substitute for using the body in active, enjoyable and demanding ways. Sports, dancing and other physical activities help maintain health and strength, as well as developing coordination and balance.

There is practically no limit to the variety of these activities, and most of them are great for you. But not all! Some people, for example,

cannot run without hurting their knees and ankles. Others are not built to swim; they just seem to sink like stones. Don't force yourself to do something that may be injurious or unpleasant. Instead, find a stimulating, healthy activity that's suitable to your physical and mental makeup. And don't be afraid to try new activities no matter what your age.

MEDICAL CONSIDERATIONS

The entire exercise program we'll outline shortly is based on the assumption that you are a healthy, injury-free individual. If you aren't, ask your doctor before undertaking any strenuous exercise. Even if you feel fine, it's a good idea to start your program with a checkup.

CARDIOVASCULAR FITNESS

The heart is a muscle. When you use it, it gets stronger. The more you demand of the heart, the more it responds. But as you grow older, the maximum rate at which your heart can beat diminishes. Since you need to exercise at 70–85% of your total capacity, the following table will tell you what your target heart rate ought to be for any age (there will, of course, be individual variations):

Age	70% of Max.	85% of Max.	Max.
25	140	170	200
30	136	165	194
35	132	160	188
40	128	155	182
45	124	150	176
50	119	145	171
55	115	140	165
60	111	135	159
65	107	130	153

TAKING YOUR PULSE

For full cardiovascular benefit, you need to maintain your target heart rate for a period of 12–20 minutes. Use your second and third fingers to check your pulse rate at the wrist. Time how many beats you feel in six seconds, then multiply by 10 to get the rate per minute.

RESISTANCE TRAINING

Muscles adapt to exercise (get stronger) when you make them contract against greater resistance than that to which they're accustomed. You can use the resistance of your own body, or the resistance provided by dumbbells and barbells.

The following is a suggested circuit of exercises designed to train the entire body. A circuit is a group of exercises done one after another without stopping.

1. Dumbbell Flyes

Lie on your back on a flat bench and rest your feet flat on the floor. Hold two dumbbells at straight arms' length directly over your chest. Your palms should be toward each other, and your elbows should be slightly bent. Keeping your arms bent, lower the dumbbells directly to the sides in an arc until the weights are below the level of the bench and you can feel a stretching sensation in your chest muscles. Bring the dumbbells back together directly above your chest by raising them upward along the same arc through which they were lowered.

This exercise firms the chest muscles. Do 10 repetitions.

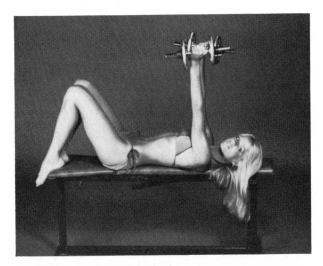

Start (above) and finish (below).

2. Incline Press

Lie back on a 45-degree incline bench and rest your feet comfortably on the floor. Hold two dumbbells at straight arms' length above your chest so that your arms are perpendicular to the floor. From this starting position, slowly bend your elbows and lower the dumbbells to touch the front part of your shoulders. As you lower the dumbbells, be certain that your upper arms go directly out to the sides and your elbows are directly under your hands at all times. Push the dumbbells back to the starting position.

This exercise fills in and shapes the upper chest area. Do 10 repetitions.

3. Barbell Curls

Grasp a barbell with a palms-up, shoulder-width grip. Stand upright, with your upper arms firmly against the sides of your torso. Keeping your upper arms motionless, bend your elbows and move the weight slowly in an arc from your thighs to your shoulders. Lower the barbell back along the same arc to the starting point. As you move the weight up and down, be sure that your upper body does not sway back and forth.

Barbell Curls trim and firm the arms. Do 10 repetitions.

Start (above) and finish (below).

Start (above) and finish (below).

4. Bent Rowing

Bend over at the waist until your torso is parallel to the floor. Grasp a barbell with a palms-down, shoulder-width grip. Bend your knees slightly to take strain off your lower back. Being sure that your upper arms travel out to the sides, pull the barbell up until it touches the lower part of your ribcage. Lower back to the start.

Bent Rowing firms and develops your upper back muscles, and helps promote better posture. Do 10 repetitions.

Start (above) and finish (below).

5. Barbell Press

Lean over and grasp a barbell with a palms-down, shoulder-width grip. Bend your legs until your hips are below shoulder level, and then use your legs to pull the barbell up to your shoulders. Tuck your elbows under the bar so the barbell is supported at the chest by your palms. From this starting position, push the weight straight up overhead until your arms are fully extended. Concentrate hard on keeping your balance. Lower the weight back to the starting point.

This exercise firms, shapes and strengthens the arms, shoulders, chest and back. Do 10 repetitions.

Start (above) and finish (below).

6. Rear Leg Kicks

Lie on your stomach, supporting yourself as shown in the photos. Keeping your leg straight, lift it up slowly as high as it will go, then lower it back to the starting position.

This exercise shapes and firms the buttocks, hips, legs and lower back. Do 20 repetitions with each leg.

7. Crunches

Lie on your back with your hands clasped behind your head. Rest your lower legs comfortably on the bench as shown. From this position, start rolling up forward, but keep your lower back on the floor. Rather than doing a Sit-up, you should attempt to force your shoulders toward your hips, shortening your torso. This will place direct tension on your frontal stomach muscles. Hold this tension for a count of two and return to the starting position.

Crunches strengthen and firm the entire midsection area. Do 20 slow repetitions.

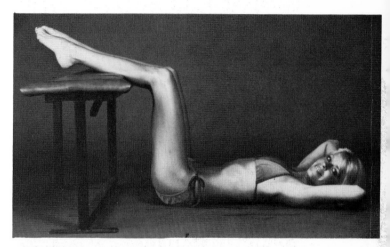

Start (above) and finish (below).

Start (above) and finish (below).

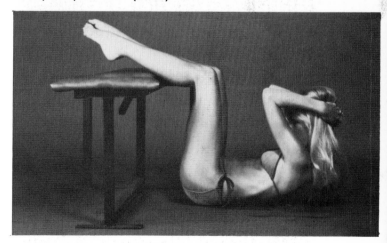

8. Twists

Stand erect with your feet spread slightly wider than shoulder width. Hold a broomstick behind your neck by grasping the ends. Slowly twist and bend toward the left until your right hand and the end of the broomstick touch your left foot. Return to the starting position and then twist to the other side.

This exercise firms, stretches and shapes the sides, hips and buttocks. Do 25 repetitions on each side.

9. Squats

Hold a barbell across your shoulders behind your neck. Stand erect and place your feet at shoulder width, your toes pointed slightly outward. Keeping your torso as upright as possible, bend your knees and sink into a squatting position. Return slowly to the start.

Be sure as you squat down that your knees travel outward directly over your feet. Squat down at least until your thighs reach a position parallel to the floor. If you have difficulty keeping your heels on the floor, rest them on a 2 × 4-inch board. Until you learn the movement, use only an unloaded barbell for resistance.

Squats are great for strengthening, shaping and developing your thighs, hips and buttocks. Do 10 repetitions.

Start (above) and finish (below).

Start (above) and finish (below).

10. Side Lunges

Stand upright with your hands on your hips and your feet spread slightly wider than shoulder width. Keeping your right leg straight, bend your left knee and dip down to the side as far as you can. Slowly straighten your left leg and return to the starting position. Repeat the movement alternately to each side.

This is a favorite leg and hip exercise of dancers, acrobats and bodybuilders. Do 10 repetitions to each side.

Start (above) and finish (below).

11. High Knees

This aerobic exercise is a variation of running in place. Begin to jog slowly in place, but lift your knees up as high as you can. As you warm up, the knees should come up even higher. Try to continue the exercise for 3–5 minutes, or longer.

This exercise firms and shapes the hips, thighs and calves.

WARM-DOWN STRETCHING

At the end of your circuit, stop to catch your breath, and then stretch out the muscles by doing the following:

A. Alternate Toe Touching

Spread your legs comfortably apart. Bend over and touch the floor, keeping your knees locked. Let your lower back stretch out for a few moments, then move your hands over to the left foot. Take hold of the ankle and pull gently. Move back over to the right and repeat the movement. Do three repetitions to each side.

B. Hamstring Stretches

Sit on the floor. Pull your knees up, and put the soles of your feet together. Hold on to your feet and try to lower your knees slowly as far as you can toward the floor. Do three repetitions.

C. Back Rows

Lie on your back, bend your knees, and place your feet flat on the floor. Push up with your body and tuck in your buttocks. Your entire body forms a kind of "bow," with only your feet and shoulders supporting you. Hold this extreme position for 3–6 seconds, come back down to the floor, then push back up again slowly, trying to increase the arch even more. Do three repetitions.

ADDITIONAL CIRCUITS

After completing an entire circuit without stopping (it may take a little time for some people to build up to that), walk around the room slowly to catch your breath. Then do another circuit. Once you have gotten used to these exercises, you should be able to do three complete circuits in 15–25 minutes.

HOW MUCH WEIGHT?

People are often confused about how much weight to use. The practical answer with this program is: don't use so much weight that you can't get through the entire program. When the weight you are using begins to feel too light and the program becomes too easy, add weight. ore

TO EACH HER OWN

Resistance training with weights is self-regulating. If you're 25 and very strong, you'll automatically use more weight than someone who is 55 and not in such good condition. The amount of weight you use is relative. The weight should be enough to test you, but it shouldn't be too much for you to handle.

HOW OFTEN?

If you limit yourself to 15–30 minutes of exercise, there is nothing to keep you from training four, five or six times a week. If you decide to double the length of the workouts, extending them to 30–60 minutes a day (which is ideal from a health and fitness standpoint), three sessions a week is adequate. Of course, you can train more often if you feel like it.

AN OUNCE OF PREVENTION

Exercise, coupled with a sound diet, can do a lot to repair the damage resulting from age and an unhealthy lifestyle. But there is a limit to the amount of repair possible once the damage has already taken place.

Gaining health, strength and fitness *before* any deterioration takes place is the ideal solution. Remember, no matter what shape you're in, any training you do now will help prevent problems in the future. And it's never too late to start. Whatever your age or athletic predisposition, treating your body the way nature intended can yield fantastic results!

Think Your Way to a Better Body

by Betty Weider

As television's Second City comedian Severn Darden once said: "Today ve vill be talking about zee universe. Vhy shpeak about zee universe? Because—zere is nozing else!"

When it comes to developing and shaping your body, "zere is nozing" better than a carefully constructed program of resistance training.

However, since you are reading this article, you probably already believe in the value of weight training. So let's go on to the next problem—given your interest, how do you go about actually developing a bodybuilding/weight training routine that meets your special needs?

THE OBSTACLE COURSE

On the surface, designing your program shouldn't be that difficult. You can refer to articles in *Muscle & Fitness*, buy one of the many bodybuilding books on the market, or join a local gym or health club.

This may sound easy, but there's a catch. First, you will be confused by the many different opinions on how to train and the different styles that various weightlifters will recommend you try. Worse, when you train at some health clubs and spas, you are given advice by employees

Dumbbell Bent Rows tone your upper back and arm muscles. From a hang position, pull the dumbbells directly up to your chest. Lower the weights back to the start.

who don't know much more than you do. These so-called "experts" are incapable of giving you good coaching when you are doing movements incorrectly.

The way around this is to become an expert yourself. Rather than just memorizing a few basic weight training rules, you need to understand the reasons these rules are important. Then, as an expert, you will have the ability to guide yourself through a training program.

FIRST THINGS FIRST

To begin with, it is necessary that you examine how bodybuilding training with weights affects the muscles. Muscles are composed of thousands of tiny fibers. Your strength is partially determined by how many muscle fibers you have and how big they are. More important, your strength also depends on how many of these fibers you are capable of using in any activity.

Each muscle works on an "all or nothing" basis—it either contracts or it doesn't. Once the muscle gets tired it will still contract, but the force of that contraction will be diminished. So, to continue doing a certain level of work, a person must use additional fibers to complete the movement.

Strength training primarily consists of adapting the nervous system so you are able to "recruit" more and more of the available muscle fibers. You force the body to call upon more of its reserves than ever before. And the subsequent adaptation involves changes such as firmness, shape, tone and strength—the important changes a person looks for when weight training.

THE RECRUITMENT TECHNIQUE

If you want your muscles to produce a great contraction, you must train with a heavier resistance. This enables you to get stronger and shapelier as you adapt to lifting the weight. This is why training with light weights and doing endless repetitions—the sort of thing taught to women in many health spas—won't do the job. The muscle gets tired, but it doesn't grow because it has not been sufficiently overloaded.

But too much weight is as counterproductive as too little. If you train with a weight that is so heavy you can lift it only a few times, the process of recruitment does not have time to take place. All you do is train your body to make use of the maximum number of fibers in a very short time. But the number of fibers you use will always be less than it would have been if you had been able to do more repetitions.

So too many repetitions doesn't work, and neither does too few. How many should you aim for? To get the answer we just have to look at what other bodybuilders have been doing for

years. Most veteran bodybuilders do 8–12 reps for the upper body and 10–15 for the lower body. You should do more repetitions with the legs than with the upper body. The lower body nervous system seems to be less efficient and, therefore, it takes a few more reps before all possible muscle fiber participation has been stimulated.

TRAINING TO FAILURE

This process of muscle recruitment won't work unless you push yourself to the point of total muscle fatigue. You have to use *all* the available fibers, and then force the body to learn to use even more. This means continuing each set until you can't do even one more repetition. If you stop short of this point you won't get the "training effect" you are seeking.

This is called "training to failure" and it will work only if you use a weight that is heavy enough. Too many beginning weight trainers decide to do 10–12 repetitions, and then stop at that point even if they could go on. That is not how training to failure works. You should lift an amount of weight that causes you to fail after 10–12 reps—no more weight, no less.

Dumbbell Curls will tone your upper arms. Keeping your upper arms motionless, curl the dumbbells in semicircles up to your shoulders.

HOW MANY SETS?

Advanced bodybuilders do anywhere from 2–5 sets per exercise and 5–20 sets per body part (and a very few do many more sets than this). But what is right for the veteran lifter is not necessarily right for the beginner.

The Nautilus company says that one set of any exercise is enough to stimulate the muscle. This may be so in theory, but it doesn't work very well in practice. For one thing, few individuals have the determination to force themselves to do an all-out effort on one set. And even if they did, the beginner's neuromuscular efficiency is not as great as the advanced bodybuilder's so it takes more time and effort for a beginner to get a training effect.

Here are some good guidelines for the beginner. The complex body parts, those that have several muscle groups (legs, back), require more sets and exercises than the simple body parts (arms). Therefore, you can plan your routines as follows:

2–4 sets per exercise.
9–12 sets for simple body parts.
12–15 sets for complex body parts.

MASS VS. DEFINITION

High reps and low weight for definition; heavy weight and low reps for mass—this is the standard advice you get. But this isn't something that needs to concern the beginner.

More repetitions burn up more calories and this will give you definition. But, compared to exercises that demand you move your whole bodyweight, weight training burns up relatively few calories. So, to get definition, you should add an aerobic activity such as running, cycling, swimming or dancing. But don't change your weight program.

HOW TO ANALYZE AN EXERCISE

Many people do exercises incorrectly because they don't fully understand the relationship between the movement and the muscle being trained. But this relationship is quite easy to grasp.

All a muscle can do is contract. If you want to understand what muscle is being trained in any movement, look to see what part of the body is doing the work.

For instance, the pectoral muscles contract to pull your arm and shoulder across the chest. This is a fairly simple function, and exercises like

Side Bends tone the muscles at the sides of your waist. Holding two light dumbbells, bend alternately from side to side.

Cable, Dumbbell or Machine Flyes and most pressing movements will work the pecs.

The functions of the biceps, on the other hand, are to curl the forearm, lift the arm, and twist the wrist and hand. Therefore, if you do an exercise that only emphasizes one of these functions, or even two, you have not worked all the muscle fibers.

Whenever you are doing a movement, consider which muscle you are training and whether or not you are forcing it to work through its entire range of motion.

HOW OFTEN TO TRAIN

The limiting factor in training is the recuperative ability of the muscle. Once you have stressed muscles, they need time to recover and adapt. If you work out before your muscles have recovered, you will slow your progress.

Some muscles recover faster than others. The biceps, for example, recover quicker than any other muscle. The spinal erectors, located in the lower back, are the slowest, taking a full 102 hours to recuperate.

You should plan your training routine so that you do not work the same muscle group two days in a row. However, you should not do a hard lower back workout more than once a week.

Here are two sample workout schedules:
Whole body: Monday, Wednesday, Friday,
  or
½ body: Monday, Thursday.
½ body: Tuesday, Friday.
The first workout involves exercising the whole body every time you train. Obviously, when you work your entire body, you will have to do less with each individual muscle.

The second type of training, called Weider Split System Training, is more practical. With it, you can train harder, and still give the body time to rest. A sample Split System routine might be:
Day 1. back, shoulders, abdominals, biceps,
       calves.
Day 2. legs, chest, abdominals, triceps,
       forearms.
Based on this, you can develop any routine that suits you. Just be sure that you always train the bigger muscles first and the smaller ones later in the session. Otherwise, the smaller muscle groups, which are usually the "weak link" when you train the bigger muscles, get too tired. Also, be sure you work your abdominals every day.

PACE

If you train too rapidly, you outrun your cardiovascular system. But if you train too slowly, your energy level drops. Try training just quickly enough so your pulse rate goes up significantly—between 120 to 140 beats per minute—and continue at this pace. Do every exercise without stopping until you have completed the workout. If you relax too much between exercises your pulse rate will drop.

MACHINES VS. FREE WEIGHTS

No bodybuilder has ever built a championship body using only machines. On the other hand, exercise devices of various sorts can be very useful in your training program. So don't get in a rut. Use all the available equipment to put some variety into your workouts. And don't let anyone sell you on using just one sort of machine, or limiting your training too severely.

Mentally and physically, the more variety you put into your workouts the better.

WHERE TO TRAIN

There have been tremendous physiques developed in poorly equipped garages. You do not need extensive facilities to do the right kind of training. But training is mental as well as physical, and the better you feel about where you train, the harder you will be able to exert yourself.

You may get more out of training at a gym than you do training at home. And it helps if that gym—or health spa, club or whatever—has a sufficient variety of equipment to keep you interested.

But if you are distracted by other members or if the employees pester you during a workout, you might want to find someplace else to train.

Take the time to find the best place available (the one that lets you do your best workout) and train there.

TRAIN THE WHOLE BODY!

When you plan your own individual training routine be sure that you include exercises that will train your whole body, every single muscle

Jumping Jacks are great for promoting general body conditioning. With your arms at your sides, spring up 6–8 inches and spread your legs 2–3 feet apart, swinging your arms up. When your feet touch the floor, immediately spring up and return to the starting position.

group. And make sure you work out at least twice a week, but not more than three times weekly.

Many male bodybuilding beginners work just on their arms and chest, and forget about the legs. Female beginners tend to do just the opposite.

Gyms are full of women training legs and ignoring the upper body. Actually women usually need less work on their legs than anywhere else. The arms, shoulders, back and chest are usually the underdeveloped areas.

If you are worried about fat thighs and hips and if you want to get your legs in terrific shape, train them along with the rest of the body. Then rely more heavily on diet to rid yourself of any extra fat you have below your waist.

THE MIND IN BODYBUILDING

There was a time when many people thought that anyone who spent time working with weights in a gym must be some sort of "dumb jock." Nowadays people are realizing that proper training involves a great deal of skill and knowledge, and that you have to use your good sense if you want to make progress.

I recommend that you learn to think about what you are doing in the gym. Don't just go through the motions. You should always try to understand why you are doing certain movements, and your workouts should be well-planned.

Weight training is the intelligent way to build up your body. And you can use your intelligence to help that training work for you.

Exercises for a Terrific Upper Body

by Stacey Bentley

"Oh no, dear," says the well-meaning but somewhat condescending male who leaps forward when he sees you reaching for a suitcase or a large bag of groceries. "That's too heavy for a little thing like you!"

Now I am as appreciative of courtesies rendered by an attentive male as anyone. But there's something in that attitude that bothers me. It's the assumption not only that women are too weak to lift anything heavier than a loaf of bread, but that this is the way things *ought* to be. As an advocate of physical fitness for both men and women, I find this assumption disturbing and dangerous.

Looking back in history, you find that the pioneer women who helped settle this country worked right alongside their men—clearing forests, planting and harvesting crops. In the Middle Ages, when the pampered spouses of the landowners whiled away the hours with needlepoint and tapestry weaving, peasant wives were out in the fields doing their share of the work.

Nobody is recommending that modern women in urban society engage in that kind of labor, but it does show what women are capable of physically. Therefore, if so many women lack the strength to take care of themselves, it would seem to be the result of social barriers rather than any natural or feminine limitations.

The fact is, women have the same structure as men, and their muscles are physiologically identical to those of the male. They're smaller, true, because of the effects of the different male and female hormones on the body. But women's muscles atrophy if they aren't used, just as men's do. And poorly conditioned muscles can adversely affect the body and internal organs in various ways.

Actually, women are not really much weaker than men in all areas of the body, just in the upper body. Composite strength scores suggest that men are 30–40% stronger than women, but the leg strength of men and women is nearly equal. In fact, when you express leg strength relative to lean body mass rather than body size, women actually score higher than men.

The reason for this disparity between upper and lower body strength in women is quite obvious. After all, the main function of the legs is to carry the body around, and women spend a lot of time on their feet just as men do. But they are discouraged early on from activities involving heavy lifting, carrying, throwing and hitting.

Bent-Over Twisting firms and tones the sides and lower back muscles. Hold a broomstick across your shoulders during the movement.

Therefore, as young men continue to gain in upper body development, women actually lose ground as they get into their 20s and beyond.

When women decide to do something about this disproportionate development of their bodies, the results can be dramatic. A relatively easy program lasting a few months can increase a woman's upper body strength by 30% or more.

In some cases, where women dedicate themselves to training, practice the proper techniques, and have the requisite genetic potential, the gains in upper body strength can be as much as 100%. Of course, women tend to shy away from this kind of training because

they've always been taught that it isn't "feminine" and—I wish I had a dollar for every time I've heard this—they think they'll develop bulging, masculine muscles.

The first objection is easily resolved. What is feminine about a woman who's 10 pounds overweight, with a protruding middle, sagging bust and flabby arms? Compare this condition to that of being strong, looking great in a bikini and passing for 29 instead of 10 years older. There's not much argument as to which is really the most feminine.

As to the issue about muscles, I yearn for the day when I can say this for the last time: large muscles come about in the presence of high testosterone levels. Women, as a rule, do not have large amounts of this hormone. This means that for the average woman, no amount of heavy weight training is going to produce more than a slight increase in muscle size.

It's true that some women have more male hormone in their system than others. This could make some difference in muscle potential. But I have watched champion male bodybuilders training over a long period. And I can tell you that those massive physiques are the result of

Pulley Pushdowns tone the triceps muscles at the back of your upper arms. From this position, slowly straighten your arms.

eight, ten or even fifteen years of the most arduous training. By following a moderate training program, the average man can expect to duplicate little of this growth. So women certainly have nothing to worry about. Believe me, getting "big" is so difficult that even the experts are constantly looking for faster, better and easier means to achieve this.

If you read *Muscle & Fitness* regularly, you'll often see photos of a new type of bodybuilder—the female variety. These women are bodybuilders in the same strict sense of the word that the men are. They spend countless hours training in the gym and then diet away as much body fat as possible to show the results of their training.

Many men and women find this look "too developed" (although the same thing has been said about the male bodybuilder for decades). But that objection should not stand in the way of the average woman improving her physique through weight training.

Few women have the motivation, dedication and physical potential to develop a competition physique. There will never be many competition bodybuilders—men or women. It's just too difficult. But what the average woman should realize is that these female bodybuilders have a lot to teach. They have learned how the body can be transformed by training, and they can pass on this knowledge to help us create the kind of bodies *we* want.

Bodybuilding can be wonderfully specific. You can use individual routines to shape, condition and firm up any area of the body you want. And this is of the utmost importance to women with their socially-induced upper body weakness. Activities like tennis, jogging or riding a bicycle won't do it.

In any sport calling for upper body strength, like volleyball or the racquet games, women find themselves at a distinct disadvantage. That is, until they recover their genetically endowed level of strength in the chest, back, arms and shoulders.

When a friend of mine interviewed a famous woman tennis player a few years ago, they got on the subject of weight training. The tennis player (whose career had begun to slide even though she was still quite young) was dead set against any kind of upper body weight training.

A little later, Billie Jean King came out in favor of more complete conditioning for tennis players, including progressive resistance training for the upper body. At an advanced age for a tennis player, and despite several knee

Dumbbell Presses are excellent for toning and strengthening your arms and shoulders. Simply push the dumbbells directly upward from the shoulders to arms' length overhead.

operations, Billie Jean is still a contender. The other woman isn't.

Women may never be as strong as men, and most of us wouldn't care to be. But strength is a by-product of conditioning. It comes with the territory. Aging involves deterioration, and proper training slows this process down. Weight training, in this sense, is a benevolent time machine.

Being stronger is also useful. Suppose that gallant who wants to carry your suitcase or bag of groceries isn't around? It's a good feeling to know you can take care of yourself. Sure, it's nice to be pampered from time to time, but how many modern women really want to return to the Victorian Age?

Weight training is good for every body. But women, with their comparative lack of upper body development, stand to benefit from it more than men. And don't worry, girls, if it suits your purposes to let that nice man help you with your baggage, go ahead. Remember, all's fair . . .

Incline Flyes stress the upper chest muscles. Keeping your arms slightly bent, begin with the dumbbells above your face. Then lower them to the position illustrated.

Hanging Knee Raises tone the lower abdominals. Start with your body completely straight and then raise your knees up to the position illustrated.

If You Do Nothing Else, Stretch

by Vicky Vodon (as told to Laura Mishima)

When women ask me for a fitness program which will make them strong, I don't limit my advice to weight training and running. "If you do nothing else," I tell them, "you must stretch."

Flexibility is the most important part of anyone's physical training program. Not only does it prevent injury, it increases one's mobility and thus enhances performance. Stretching is a means of relaxing your muscles. Think of it as the dessert at the end of a good meal, the reward for your productive workout. Treat yourself to at least 20 minutes of stretching each day.

Stretching keeps the body in balance. It lengthens the muscles and gives them time to relax. What a contrast to the constant force placed upon a muscle during a heavy weight workout or endurance running. It's a non-contracting exercise which must be done at a slow, static, free-flowing pace. It should be enjoyable.

"There just isn't time," you might say. "Two hours of weight training or running five miles is enough of a workout." I disagree.

The more you train, the more energy you expend—the more you need to stretch. There is a direct relationship between well-developed

muscles and stiffness. To avoid stiffness and resulting injury, the correct amount of flexibility must be attained.

It's like a recipe for a pie crust. If it calls for one cup of sugar for every two cups of flour, when you double the recipe, you must double the quantities of each ingredient. Twenty minutes of stretching is required for every 40 minutes of strenuous physical activity. I can't overemphasize the importance of allowing sufficient time to relax and stretch your muscles before and after a workout. It's like preventive medicine that will pay big dividends in the future.

"But why should it take more than 10 minutes?" you say. "It shouldn't take longer than that to perform 'x' number of positions, then hold."

Just as in weight training, it's not what you do but how you do it. Stretching requires a certain amount of concentrated effort. You must give your muscles time to relax and lengthen. If force is placed on the muscles—such as bouncing or some ballistic movement—they will automatically contract. It's a natural defense mechanism which takes place in the Golgi-tendon apparatus (stretch receptive fibers).

To avoid stiffness and contraction, flexibility exercises must consist of a slow, static stretch. The average session should last at least 20 minutes, although ideally stretching and that physical activity should be done on a 1:2 ratio. Concentrate on working a few major muscle groups and hold each position for 30–60 seconds. Never force a position and breathe normally when you stretch. Strive for a deep breathing meditation similar to yoga.

The more you stretch, the greater your range of motion. When exercises are done in a more complete range of motion, they require less flexibility. You become naturally more flexible and therefore more efficient. It becomes easier for you to exercise.

When your athletic event or weight training program calls for a particular response—lifting more weight or sprinting at a faster pace—your flexibility will allow you to respond. But if your range of motion is restricted, you're more likely to strain a muscle. The stiffness of contracting muscles may not result in immediate injury, but cumulative stiffness will eventually haunt you and hinder your performance.

To get the most out of your flexibility workout, pay particular attention to sequence. If your back is inflexible, it will most likely hamper the flexibility of your other body parts. Tight hamstrings when you attempt to touch your toes may be due to a stiff back—not the hamstring muscles alone.

I recommend a series of stretches that start from the center of the body—and work out to the limbs. At least 7 to 10 minutes of your entire stretching program should focus on the area around the spine. You'll be surprised at how you can improve the flexibility of your legs by simply stretching the back.

Continue to stretch the major muscle groups—the legs, hamstrings, quadriceps, triceps, biceps and pectoralis major muscles. Finally work down to the ankles and calves. Concentrate on performing a slow, fluid, relaxed movement. Stretching not only increases one's potential in athletic performance—it relieves stress and serves as emotional as well as physical therapy.

Here are a few stretching exercises which should serve as a framework for your stretching program. As you experiment with the illustrated exercises, don't be afraid to incorporate new stretches and individualize the exercises to fit your needs. Once you develop a patterned routine, your stretching workout will become automatic and the time you spend stretching will be meditative. Flexibility will be a reward—something to look forward to—as well as a means of improving performance, preventing injury and achieving peace of mind!

1. Premier Stretch

From a standing position, feet shoulder-distance apart, slowly bend forward at the waist to stretch the hamstrings. Relax and feel an easy stretch in your lower back. Remember to bend the knees slightly. Then, clasp hands together behind the back and pull hands up to stretch the shoulders.

Model for all exercises except the Spider: Candy Csencsits, Ms. Eastern America.

2. The Catcher

From the first position, bend knees slowly and assume squat position. Feet should point out with heels on the ground. If you have trouble balancing in this position, support yourself by outstretching the arms and grasping a fixed object—like a baseball catcher does. This exercise will stretch the ankles, Achilles tendon, groin and lower back.

3. Groin Stretch

From exercise two, roll down slowly onto buttocks. Put soles of feet together with hands around feet, and pull yourself forward to stretch the groin and back. Keep elbows on outside of legs for stability. No bouncing!

4. Knees to Chest

Lie on back with knees pulled to chest. Pull buttocks off the ground slightly. Head should remain on the floor in a relaxed position.

One at a time: Then straighten both legs, relax and pull left leg to chest. Keep back of head on the mat, but don't strain. Feel an easy stretch. Repeat with right leg.

Cross-over: Straighten left leg and hold right knee to chest. With left hand, pull bent leg up and over opposite leg (as shown in photo). Both shoulders should remain on the floor, and right arm should be outstretched in the opposite direction. Your left hand controls the stretch in the lower back and gluteus muscles by pulling the top leg towards the floor. Repeat exercise to the other side.

5. Bottoms Up

Lie on your back in a legs-over-head position. Keep knees straight and hands on back of hips for balance. Find a comfortable position and relax. If it's more comfortable, knees may be slightly bent. Do not strain.

Toe touch: Clasp feet with hands and feel a stretch in the lower back, hamstrings and Achilles tendon.

Roll-down: Roll down slowly, keeping legs straight, trying to lower one vertebra at a time. Hands should be behind ankles with knees bent slightly for a more controlled stretch. Practice to achieve that slow motion. Keep head on mat and repeat the entire series.

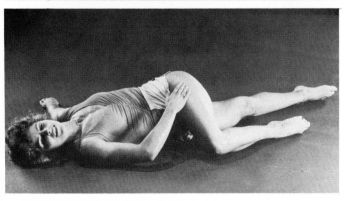

6. Twister

With right leg straight, put left foot flat on the floor on the other side of right knee. Reach over left leg with right arm, so that your elbow is on the outside of left leg. With left hand resting on the ground behind you, slowly turn head to look over left shoulder. Bend right elbow and gently push against bent leg. This stretches the gluteus and internal and external obliques. Repeat to the opposite side.

7. Variation Hurdler's Stretch

In seated position, left leg straight and toes up, place right leg bent so that sole of foot tucks inside upper part of straight leg (see photo). Lean slightly forward and stretch hamstring.

Side variation: Sit straight, then bend over sideways grasping toes with left hand and pull towards you. Slowly arch right arm up and over torso towards left foot. This exercise stretches the hamstrings, Achilles, obliques and lateral back.

8. The Spider

Lie on stomach and pull lower legs towards buttocks from top of foot for better leverage.

The arch: Hyper-extend back by pulling foot in upward direction with arms. This stretches the pectoralis major muscles as well as the quadriceps.

Model: Lynn Conkwright, World Bodybuilding Champion.

9. Sunrise Salute

Stand with arms stretched overhead, hands clasped and fingers pointing up. Stretch upward concentrating on totally lengthening your body frame. Take a deep breath and release slowly.

The bend: Bend over at the waist. Grab back of ankles pulling forehead to the knees. This stretches the upper hamstrings and back.

The lunge: Place hands on floor on either side of foot, and bend both knees extending the right leg towards the back of the body. Clasp hands together, arms overhead, and looking straight up, raise torso to erect position.

10. The Retreat

Place hands back on floor beside bent knee. Pull bent leg back beside straight leg and press heels of foot to floor with legs straight and head pushed down between shoulders. This will stretch the Achilles tendon, hamstrings and shoulder girdle.

Lowering: Bend knees slowly, bend arms and lower chest towards floor by pushing chin forward just above mat level until arms become straightened.

Another arch: Arch back with head to ceiling. Legs should be straightened and spread apart approximately shoulder distance.

The prayer: Keeping arms straight, pull buttocks from mat and slowly assume sitting position over feet. Toes should be pointed with buttocks resting on feet.

Giving Mother Nature a Boost for the Bust

by Betty Weider

The advertisement reads, "Wanna be guaranteed a voluptuous bustline? Here's the fool-proof way to add inches to your bust . . ."

It's a lucrative business, because in today's society, an attractive bust is a must. For some of today's styles, if you don't have enough of it, you simply can't wear it. And if your stuff sags, it's got to be a drag. I mean, if you can't keep it up, you'd better get a bigger cup. Look at the variety of brassieres on the market today.

Some padded bras, designed to push-you-up or fill-you-out, will compensate for what you lack. At the other extreme, those who are over-endowed can take comfort in bras that smooth and flatten as well as support. There are hidden flaps and bras without straps, front-fastening hooks and a variety of looks.

Then, there are the gimmicks you find in the back of most women's magazines. Exercisers that add inches; creams and massage treatments which are made to stimulate growth. Imagine, tricking Mother Nature like that. Beware!

Unless the advertisement was written by old Mother Nature herself, there's got to be a catch. All the stuffing in the world won't compensate for a flat chest. The support-type bras will smother your breasts, but if you're overweight, you know your fate. Even the most exotic and expensive creams lack the growth hormones necessary for a bigger bust. Most exercisers add inches to the bustline, not the breasts. Unless Mother Nature intended for you to be stacked, there are limits to your potential.

Rather than invest in an assortment of brassieres and bust-developing products, the Weider Research Clinic suggests that you invest some time in yourself. Instead of pushing-up or covering-up what you don't like, learn what you can do to make the most of what you've got. Since you can't very well change what your mother had and what your father's mother had not, set goals that are realistic. Accept the fact that your bustline is a matter of genetics, but then do all you can to bring your bustline up and out to its maximum potential by beautifying and shaping what nature gave you. Then, follow my advice in these three areas:

1. *Nutrition*—It is impossible to look beautiful if your diet is poor. The right diet can provide 85% of your success in body shaping.
2. *Exercise*—The breast is comprised primarily of adipose or fat tissue, but by strengthening its surrounding muscles—mainly the pectoralis

major muscle—you can improve its shape and position.

3. *Posture*—By standing tall, with shoulders back, head high and stomach in, you automatically uplift the breast and enhance your overall appearance.

Actually, the principles of bustline development are not so different from the principles of physical fitness. To look and feel your best, the Weider Research Clinic recommends a combination of rest, exercise and nutrition. For bustline development, it's a matter of posture, too. A closer look at the breast's

Cable Crossovers are an excellent movement for the chest muscles. Simply pull the cable handles downward in semicricles until your hands touch each other a few inches in front of your hips.

basic anatomy will support our theory. The most dominant feature of the breast is a collection of spongy-like fatty deposits that surround the breast. These deposits are the primary factor in the determination of the size of the breast.

Since breast size is a matter of fat content in the mammary glands and milk ducts, there's no way to increase the breast itself without gaining weight. But by strengthening and thus thickening the pectoralis major muscle, you can improve the breast's shape and position. Furthermore, the development of these muscles will encourage a consciousness about body posture. By stretching the ribs and training yourself to stand proud, your bustline and overall appearance is enhanced.

Besides the pectoralis major muscle, there are ten other muscles which influence the total picture: the latissimus dorsi, the serratus anterior, the teres major and minor, the trapezius, the pectoralis minor, the infraspinatus, the rhomboideus major and minor and the obliquus abdominis externus. A study of bodybuilding literature may lead to other methods of weight training and exercises designed to facilitate strength and development in these areas.

IF YOU'RE OVERWEIGHT

Underlying body development and improvement is nutrition. It's impossible to look your best if you're not eating right. If you're overweight, fat is distributed throughout your body, including your breasts. More than likely, the excess weight will cause sagging breasts, blouses with buttons that pop open and a bouncing bosom when you walk.

Your first step is to lose weight by eating the minimum amount of essential proteins and low-carbohydrate foods. Try to keep your carbohydrate intake to around 40 grams per day and draw from natural sources like vegetables and fruit. An inexpensive calorie book, found at supermarket counters and bookstores, is both helpful and necessary for the conscientious dieter. Usually a daily intake of between 900 and 1500 calories is safe for weight reduction. If you are extremely overweight or have some medical problem, it is always best to see a doctor before restricting your present diet.

In addition to losing weight, you want to firm and strengthen the muscles supporting your chest. Therefore, your exercise program will consist of higher repetitions and more training days. Exercise your chest muscles three times a week instead of two. A woman who is overweight might perform these two exercises, and then follow through with a giant set of four exercises.

1. Cable crossovers: four sets of 15.
2. Dumbbell pullovers: four sets of 15.

The Weider Giant Sets for Bustline Development are performed one after the other with no pause. Do each exercise for 12–15 repetitions. By failing to pause between exercises, you are utilizing the Weider Giant Set principle, which helps burn fat faster and shapes your bustline tissue. As you get stronger and more advanced, you can repeat a giant set twice, and eventually three times. Make progress slowly—the important thing here, as in any exercise program, is *consistency*.

IF YOU'RE UNDERWEIGHT

These women have the opposite problem. They're considerably underweight and most of them have no bustline to speak of. A flat-chested woman's goal is to develop her bustline and improve the general fitness of her body.

When most women try to lose weight, one of the first places it comes off seems to be the breasts. Gaining weight is a different story. It's harder to direct the extra pounds to a desired area. If you're like most women, your upper body is comparatively weaker than your lower body. Thus, the pectoralis major muscle and its surrounding muscles are underdeveloped.

In addition to the following exercises, which the Weider Research Clinic has put together for women who want to develop their bustline, a diet high in protein will help. You can gain weight by eating more calories, carbohydrates and fats, but remember that one of the prime constituents of muscle is protein. Bodybuilders on a strict competitive program generally try to consume one gram of protein daily for each pound of body weight.

Foods like milk, eggs, meat and poultry are "complete" proteins. They contain all eight amino acids esssential for protein synthesis. A protein supplement, especially one containing the same protein-to-fat ratio as the breast, is recommended whether your goal is to gain weight or simply to improve firmness. Fluctuations in weight will be determined by the food you consume besides the protein mix.

A well-balanced diet is the basis from which your bustline and physical fitness can grow. Gaining weight will help fill out your breasts, and the following exercises are a means to the end. Think of improved posture as the mandatory, finishing touch.

If you're just beginning to discover the world of exercise and weight training, the following weight program done twice weekly is a good start:

1. Bench press: three sets of 10 (alternate between incline and flat movements).
2. Dumbbell flyes: three sets of 10.
3. Single dumbbell pullovers: three sets of 10.

Some of the modern gyms now have a butterfly machine, which works each side by pushing the weight forward (with each arm held

Pec Deck Flyes strongly contract the pectoral muscles. If this machine isn't available, you can substitute regular Flat-Bench Flyes using two dumbbells.

at a 90 degree angle) from the side to the front of the body. Again, three sets of 10 is an excellent start, adjusting the weight to whatever poundage is comfortable.

If you're underweight, do all the exercises but pause about 30 seconds to one minute between each exercise. Do each exercise 8–10 times and try increasing the resistance as quickly as possible. Exercise twice weekly, not three times. Your goal is to *build* tissue.

IF YOUR WEIGHT IS NORMAL

If your weight is normal, congratulations. Not only for maintaining a healthy level of weight, but for not being satisfied with merely weighing a normal weight. You realize that your body needs more shape than a normal figure—normal implies average, and who wants to get lost in the crowd?

Since you have no weight problem, keep eating healthy, nutritious foods. Your diet probably consists of high protein foods, with a minimum of carbohydrates—maybe 60 grams daily. The exercise program I recommend should not cause you to gain excessive weight. But the effects you will get from toning and strengthening your body may change your life.

Exercise will improve your posture, raise your bustline and firm the total area. This combination will greatly improve the total appearance of your bustline, especially when your waistline measures less from the routines you've been doing.

You need not exercise your bustline more than twice weekly, but if you're in fairly good shape, you may want to try the following advanced bustline program.

In this exercise program, there are two stages. The first is a warm-up period, and the second is the actual exercise program.

Before you start the actual bust-developing exercises, do the two warm-up movements, and make sure you do not rest or cool down between the warm-ups and the actual exercises.

Warm-Up #1: ARM CIRCLES—This is not only an excellent warm-up, but it also helps uplift the bustline as well as trim the upper arm. Stand erect with arms held horizontally to each side. Without bending elbows or wrists, describe fairly large circles with your hands. Do 30 repetitions, then reverse the direction of the circles and do 30 more reps.

Warm-Up #2: PUSHUPS WITH KNEES BENT— Get on your hands and knees on the floor.

Keeping your knees bent and on the floor, do pushups. Begin with one set of 10 and eventually work up to three sets of 10 by trying to add one repetition a day or one set each week. Eventually, you will be strong enough to do men's pushups—legs straight and knees locked.

WEIDER GIANT SET BUST-DEVELOPER EXERCISES

When you have completed these warm-ups, move promptly into the following exercise routine. These following four exercises are done in what is called a Giant Set manner. In other words, the exercises are done in sequence without resting between exercises. Always precede the first Giant Set of exercises with the two warm-up movements described above.

Exercise #1: FLAT FLYES—Lie on your back on a bench with feet planted firmly on the floor. Hold a dumbbell or heavy book in each hand with arms extended straight above your head. Keeping arms straight (do not bend at elbows), extend them as far down as possible to each side. For starters, repeat 10 times. As you increase your strength and are able to do this exercise with relative ease, increase the amount of weight and/or repetitions.

Exercise #2: BARBELL PRESS OR DUMBBELL PRESS ON BENCH—Again, lie on your back on the bench and press the barbell or dumbbell up from your chest as you would on a bench press machine. If using dumbbells, be sure to keep the weights level at all times. Start out with a comfortable weight, but don't be afraid to increase the poundage as you increase your strength. Control is very important in this exercise—the motion should be slow and fluid for 10 repetitions.

Start.

Finish.

Exercise #3: FLAT PULLOVER WITH DUMBBELLS ON BENCH—Lie on your back on the bench with feet planted firmly on the floor. Using one dumbbell or book, hold it straight-armed above your head with both hands. Then, lower the weight back as far as possible, getting a good stretch, and return slowly to the overhead starting position. Do 10 repetitions.

Start.

Finish.

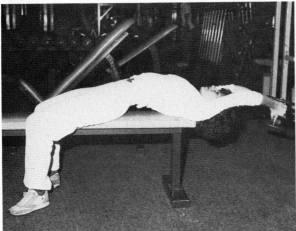

Exercise #4: INCLINE PRESS ON BENCH—This exercise is similar to #2 except that you should use a bench adjusted to a 45-degree angle. This will work the upper pectoralis muscles and uplift your firmer bustline. Again, do 10 repetitions.

Start (above) and finish (below).

Your goal in the Giant Set program is to be able to run through this series of four exercises three times, non-stop. In other words, do the four exercises, then repeat them, and repeat again. You may have to build up to this three-series level gradually, but always keep it as a goal.

A final reminder: exercises should be performed with both enthusiasm and common sense. If you can't do all the required repetitions, then do each exercise with fewer repetitions; *but do all exercises!* They work all areas of the bustline.

Don't get so ambitious and do so many exercises the first day that you find it painful to move the next day. To maintain your beautiful new bustline, you'll have to continue these exercises (twice weekly) and maintain good eating habits.

Don't forget that finishing touch: *good posture.* These are a number of isometric exercises which promote good posture, but the only one who can provide it is you. Look in the *mirror* and practice standing straight, waist in, bust out. Because you care about yourself and your appearance, others are bound to notice. You'll no longer need to thumb through the back pages of those women's magazines looking for gimmicks to improve your bustline—now you'll be the walking advertisement!

Parallel Bar Dips strongly stress the chest, shoulders, and triceps muscles. From this position, simply push your arms straight. Lower back down to the starting point and repeat the movement.

The Slim, Firm Waistline

by Mandy Tanny

I didn't always look as good as I do now. Two years ago after nine months of pregnancy, I looked at my stomach and couldn't believe it would ever be in shape again. It was so darn big.

It looked like I was carrying two watermelons in there. I watched the stretch marks appear, and every day they would get bigger and bigger. My stomach was so heavy I literally had to carry it around. That stomach can get pretty big, and some women get scared thinking it might never go down.

My fears were somewhat allayed when I looked around me and saw other women with children who had regained their former figures. On second thought, I realized that they hadn't gone back to the way they were. They merely covered up the traces of pregnancy with clothes.

Two weeks after I had my own baby, I was as big as ever with big rolls of flab that actually overlapped around my stomach. That's when I decided to get to the nearest gym.

I faced a hard cruel image. Even after the baby was born. I didn't lose a lot of weight. In fact I began to *gain* again, and I tipped the scales at 160 pounds. I was scared.

Dismal thoughts went through my mind. It seemed like there was no hope. When I first got

Mandy Tanny, a mother in her thirties, shows remarkable shape and physical condition.

to the gym, I was so paranoid that I immediately started working on my stomach. As time went on and I dieted, I began losing that weight. But instead of losing the excess in my waist, my waist remained thick from the hundreds of full situps I was doing every day.

I did three or four different kinds of ab work along with those full situps, and my waist grew thicker as I got thinner. I worked out five days a week, and after realizing what was happening, I cut down my ab work. I really didn't know where to go from there—the abs weren't going back into shape the way I was hoping they would.

I began to realize that a lot of it had to do with my diet. As time went on and I lost more and more flab in that area, I noticed some soft skin that was never there before. I had two goals—tighten the skin and streamline the midsection muscle. That meant I had to diet harder and look for a different way to work my midsection.

With a certain sense of loss, I abandoned leg raises, roman chair situps, full situps and twists. I replaced them with "crunches," the well-known favorite of bigtime male bodybuilders. My waist

grew smaller—the system was working.

Between the altered diet and the crunches, as time went on I achieved definition. It didn't happen overnight. Nine months after the baby was born, it started happening.

Inspired by that time, I continued with driving workouts day after day. Then I noticed something else: veins showing through on my lower abs. I couldn't believe it was happening to me. Everything that I had done was right. Today, two years later, I use the vascularity on my lower abs as a barometer of my condition.

The longer I train now, the less time I need to spend on my abs. The most striking transitions took place during the past two years. Initially it was a matter of losing that excess flab. After that I had to trim down the waist. That was followed by definition, and finally by vascularity—the mark of ultimate condition.

It makes you wonder how much farther you can go, and it certainly proves it can be done. All that from someone who gave birth to a 10-pound kid.

My ab work now consists of two sets of concentrated crunches every time I work out. I lie flat on my back on the floor with my calves

Seated Twisting firms your entire waistline. Hold a broomstick across your shoulders during the movement.

Crunches—Start (above) and finish (below).

resting across a bench press bench, knees bent at a right angle. I do one set of 30 reps with my legs apart, and one set of 30 reps with my legs together. The feet hang loose.

There is a lot of technique to be learned in doing concentrated squeezes. Don't put the hands behind the head because the swinging elbows tend to give you too much upward momentum. Put your arms in front of you or down at your sides. Your head too can cause upward momentum if you throw it forward as you raise up. Start the movement from the lower spine and shift to the back and nape of the neck. Mainly, don't start the movement by throwing the head forward. Tension should remain on the abs from start to finish.

I consider these crunches a key exercise. It has become very popular, particularly in the health spas these days. After 50 years of inefficient methods of training, women's gyms are finally getting around to abdominal movements whose effectiveness must be credited to the training methods of modern musclemen. Most of what any of us know must be credited to tried and proven bodybuilding principles.

However, women still do the traditional, full situps. They demonstrate it on TV exercise shows—an exercise that should have been rejected with the bustle. I'm not saying that full situps have no value. They helped me right after I had my baby, when my abdominals were stretched and soft. These muscles hadn't been used in a long time, and full situps toned them a lot. Apart from those conditions, however, surface abdominal muscle work is best.

I am also a jogger. During my second year of comeback training, I was jogging three miles every day on an electric treadmill in the gym prior to my workout. The jogging contributed to my abdominal definition. When I would miss a few days of jogging, I noticed that the vascularity would disappear.

I averaged four jogging days a week, three miles a day. It was a contributing factor to a sleek midsection. Even today when I stop jogging for a while, I notice that smoothness returning. No one else sees it, but I do. I'll notice that a couple of those delicate veins have gone into hiding, and I have to go fetch them again.

Dieting of course is basic to bodybuilding. All the training in the world amounts to nothing if you can't see your body for the fat encasing it. If you are fat and you don't diet, reading this article is a waste of time.

The only difference between women's and men's bodybuilding is diet. Men adjust their diets for maximum muscle growth. They need more protein for that, and they eat more frequently. Women want the sleek look supported by good substantial muscle. A woman eating an average amount of food every day and working out with weights would likely get pretty husky. Since most women who bodybuild prefer to look slender and muscular—no, not slender, rather animal-like—they cannot eat the way others do. Separation from the ordinary is dependent on diet as well as training.

There is a lot of natural, supportive muscle in a woman's midsection. All she has to do is lose the fat and peak the muscle by using the right kind of exercise to bring out the definition. The problem with most women's stomachs is not a lack of muscle, but rather too much fat. Women can look sensational with defined abs. As a rule, muscle won't make the waist big, but if definition is visible, the chances are the woman has very little body fat—little body fat means a trim waist.

Good abdominal development can be accomplished with minimal exercise. When you are striving for definition rather than size, you don't need a lot of strenuous ab work, just the right kind of it. As multi-purpose muscles, the abdominals are naturally, fairly well developed. Exercise as I've described it helps peak that available development.

Unless you have some athletic purpose for developing the deep hip flexors that are not visible, it is best to stick with the surface muscles. In that way you will maintain a small waist, but with definition. The deep abdominal muscles as aiding synergists will be firmed by surface activity just the same.

Firmness and definition will help eliminate the "pot-bellied" look. One could very well use plain situps to gain size and strength. My own waist was strong and hard from years of ballet work, but when I did situps I found they increased my waist an inch-and-a-half—size I didn't need at the time I was trying to reduce.

As far as I am concerned, the great variety of abdominal exercises generally taught to women do one thing—nothing. The major mistake is not learning how to concentrate while working the abs. Most women rely on momentum and "body English" to do the exercises and fail to focus on the object of their desire. They'll get as much good out of disco dancing.

Some also hook their feet under something for leverage when they do abdominal raises, which

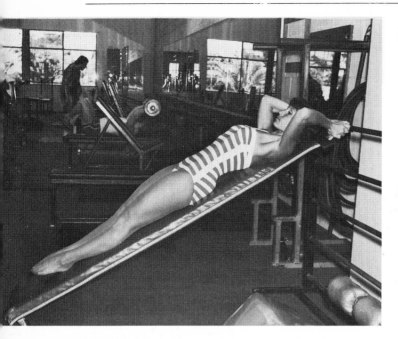 

makes the exercise easier. With the feet free as in crunches, the work falls entirely on the abdominal muscles. Crunches are to a woman's abs what the dumbbell concentration curl is to a man's biceps: they develop peak muscularity.

Why did I allow myself to weigh 160 pounds in the first place? Like I said, I was pregnant. I knew I wasn't supposed to eat for two, but it was fun to think that way.

I was a housewife living in a remote part of

Hawaii for years, one step ahead of the encroaching torpor of the tropics that engulfs the unwary. I had stopped training completely. Then one day, I awoke to the devastation all around me, and there I was right in the middle of it, being introduced by fate at a body weight of 160 pounds: Mandy versus Her Avoirdupois.

Thanks to bodybuilding, I won out. Everything's back to normal. Oh, *better than normal* because I've even got definition now!

Building a Shapely, Sensuous Back

by Lisa Lyon (as told to Laura Mishima)

When a woman looks in the mirror, her attention is usually directed at the face, hair, thighs, hips, waist and bust. Society has placed great emphasis on facial makeup, hair products and fashionable clothing to cover up an out-of-shape body. Whatever a woman's problem area with her body, I think it's safe to say that her last consideration is the back.

My priorities differ from those of most women, because as I've often said, I want my body to contrast from the average woman's. I train to achieve definition and shapeliness in my back. To me, there's a certain sensuality in the curvature of a well-developed lower back. A strong, supportive back also improves posture and enhances your overall physical health.

The back and spine are the basis of good posture, circulation and, therefore, a healthy appearance. Older women often complain about back problems, particularly if they're overweight. When you ignore the back region, you're really neglecting your entire body structure.

Sagging stomachs and sunken chests can be attributed to poor posture, even if your weight is normal. The best-built body, if held improperly, will get lost in the crowd.

In addition to enhancing your physical

Lisa Lyon won the first Women's World Bodybuilding Championship in 1979.

appearance, a strong back improves the nervous system. Chiropractors stress the importance of maintaining proper back alignment. In the same sense that the heart is the center of your body's circulatory system, the spine is the core of your nervous system. A weak back can lead to limited mobility in other areas. A strong, shapely back creates a proud, dignified line.

I realize that most women don't want a muscular lat spread or trapezius. My goal is ultimate tone and definition, but if you merely want to condition and strengthen your back to enhance general fitness, do the same exercises I do but use lighter weights. By opening up your rib cage and providing additional support for the spinal column, you will have improved the durability of your entire body.

My back workout includes six basic exercises: four for the upper back, and two for the lower region. The first four exercises will work your latissimus dorsi and trapezius muscles. As you do the exercises, concentrate on the muscles you are working. The last two exercises will affect that sexy lower back.

Russian weightlifters say that the lower back is the center of power. Not only does the lower back provide alternate support for the legs during heavy lifts, it supplements abdominal training, thus reducing menstrual and digestive problems.

If you're a beginner, I recommend following the exact order and procedure of these exercises. But once you have mastered good form and are making considerable gains, feel free to use the Weider Instinctive Training Principle. Without deviating from my goals, I adapt my program and gear it towards my day-to-day feelings.

I must also consider the availability of equipment. If a machine is occupied or broken, I either improvise or innovate a new exercise, working the same body parts in different ways. Training at a busy gym like Gold's, I learned right away the need for flexibility in training. Unless you can afford a home gym, be prepared to adapt to the community spirit and don't let it interfere with the intensity of your training.

The only time a beginner should deviate from the workout sequence I've set out here is when supersetting two exercises. For instance, do 8–10 repetitions of one exercise followed by 8–10 reps of another exercise, then return to the original exercise and begin a second set. This is done with positive results on many pull-down/pull-up exercise combinations.

Finally, proper breathing is essential in order to expand the rib cage. Practice inhaling on the pulling movement and exhaling on the release.

Your muscles need oxygen to function and grow, and if you hold your breath or breathe unnaturally, you deny them that freedom. Breathe at a relaxed pace until it becomes second nature. Once your breathing is in harmony with your movements, you can focus on exercise technique and muscle growth.

A woman's strength is determined in part by her previous upper body conditioning. Therefore, it's hard for me to dictate what poundages you should use. Let reason dictate how much you should lift for how many reps. If you can perform the required number of sets and reps using good technique and controlling each movement, then increase the weight and follow the same procedure.

To work the inner muscles, use a close grip; to exercise the outer muscles, try a wide grip. The first four exercises utilize this principle.

1. Wide-Grip Lat Pulldowns

Sit on a stool facing the lat pulldown machine and find a comfortable weight which you can pull down without arching your back or straining. Use only the back muscles and arms to pull the weight down. Alternately bring the bar forward to the base of the neck and back to the ridge of the shoulder. Keep the body stable and don't let the weight fly back to its starting position. Do 4–6 sets of 8–10 repetitions.

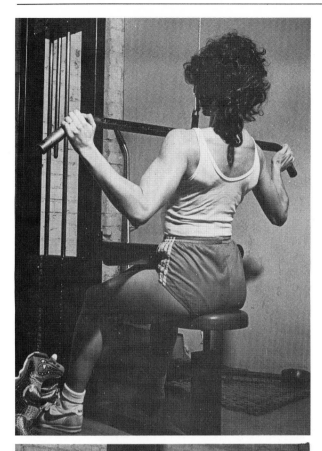

2. Low-Pulley Rowing

Using a V-handled bar, place your hands in a steering-wheel position and brace your feet on the bar in front for support (see photo). Pull the weight up using the back muscles only, rather than your entire body weight. Pull the bar back to the lower ribs, then extend out, stretching the body forward. Feel a full stretch in the lats. Do three or four sets of 10 reps. Start with about 50 pounds and increase the weight at your own pace.

3. Close-Grip Underhand Pulldown

Again, position yourself at the pulldown station, but this time use a narrow, less-than-shoulder-width grip and turn your hands inward. Extend your arms until you feel a full stretch at the top, then pull the weight down to below the breast. Strive for a full range of motion for three or four sets of 8–10 repetitions. Superset this exercise (or follow it) by . . .

4. Wide-Grip Barbell Rowing

Stand on a six-inch block, and use a wider-than-shoulder-width grip. Bend at the waist, keeping your back parallel to the floor. Using a very light weight or even an unloaded bar, bend the knees slightly and pull the weight up to the bottom of your rib cage while assuming the bent-over position. Lower the weight with control to a point below the feet and feel a stretch at the bottom of the movement. Remember to utilize proper breathing techniques throughout. Do three sets of 10 reps.

5. Hyperextensions

This is my favorite lower back exercise and I do four sets of 25 repetitions. Using the hyperextension apparatus, start from a 90-degree angle, lying face down, and raise your upper torso to an angle slightly greater than 180 degrees (or parallel to the floor). Practice control while raising and lowering your body. When you can perform high repetitions without strain, increase the difficulty of this exercise by holding a plate behind your head.

6. Good Mornings

Hold the barbell behind your shoulders, using a comfortable grip. Stand with your feet together or slightly apart and your knees slightly bent. With your head up, bend forward to a 90-degree angle, then return to the starting position. On this particular exercise, there is no need to use heavy weight and run the risk of straining the lower back. Use light weights or no weight at all on the bar. Do three sets of 8–10 repetitions.

I've already reviewed the benefits of a strong, shapely, well-developed back. Let me, in conclusion, caution you against back injuries. Since the spine is the center of your nervous system, you must take precautions whenever lifting heavy objects. Of course, the back routine I've presented here will help you strengthen and condition your back for such feats. Still, be careful!

Now, on a positive note, don't forget the improved circulation and better posture which will result from doing this routine! And I still say a streamlined lower back is sexy! Wouldn't you agree?

Try My Ms. Olympia Shoulder Workout

by Rachel McLish

My deltoids weren't very developed until I hit upon a super routine for that body part about a year ago. Within three months my shoulders had much better shape and contour. And by the time I won the US Women's Bodybuilding Championships last April, they had become proportionate to the rest of my body. I considered it a great personal victory!

After that I slipped into another (less effective) shoulder routine. When I failed to win the Zane invitational in June, I re-evaluated myself. It seemed as though the judges liked outstanding deltoid development, as well as very sharp muscularity, neither of which I had at the time. So I decided to go back to my old routine in an effort to add more muscle mass to my deltoids. I resolved to diet even longer and more strictly than I had before. And, finally, I decided to spend more time in the hot Texas sun to develop a super-dark tan.

As you probably know, this plan paid off handsomely with a Ms. Olympia title and the prize money that went with it. And while I'd like to save my dietary secrets for a later article, I do want to share with you the methods I used to increase my shoulder development so dramatically and quickly.

Radiant Rachel McLish has won the Ms. United States and Ms. Olympia titles.

Above all else, I need high-intensity workouts since that's the only type of training that improves my muscle size. In general, I like to use pre-exhaustion, partial reps, heavy weights and the Weider Slow, Continuous Tension Training Principle in my workouts.

Specifically, I begin my shoulder routine with a warm-up cycle of Side Laterals, Presses and Bent Laterals, one set (15–20 reps) of each exercise with light weights. Such a warm-up is essential because the shoulder joints and deltoid muscles

With six years of heavy resistance workouts behind her, Rachel developed what many consider to be the world's best women's bodybuilding physique.

With Machine Side Laterals, simply raise your arms out to the sides as high as possible. Pause for a moment at the top, then lower back to the start.

seem to be more susceptible to injury than any other area of the body. But don't worry about this; with a good warm-up there's very little chance of incurring an injury.

After the warm-up, I do three supersets of Side Laterals and Overhead Presses, 6–8 reps per set with the heaviest weights I can handle in strict form. On one or two sets of each movement I'll also do some partial reps in the contracted position to add some extra intensity.

The Side Laterals pre-exhaust my deltoids before the Presses, so supersetting these two exercises dramatically increases the intensity of a workout. Pre-exhaustion allows me to do less total sets per body part, which saves me valuable time in each workout. Instead of having to train 1½–2 hours per day, I can finish my workout in 45–60 minutes. When you're as busy as I've been lately, this can be a real blessing.

The club at which I train has mostly Dyna-Cam machines, which I personally endorse. Ordinarily I superset my Side Laterals and Shoulder Presses on these machines. But when I'm traveling— which I seem to be doing much more frequently nowadays—I use free weights for these two

movements, or I even do them on Nautilus machines. You can, in fact, use free weights if machines aren't available; you'll sacrifice nothing in terms of either training intensity or results.

Side Laterals work the medial (side) heads of my deltoids, while the Presses work primarily the anterior (frontal) deltoid heads. This leaves only the posterior (rear) deltoid heads to be trained, so my final deltoid exercise is Dumbbell Bent Laterals (or Rear Laterals on a machine), which stresses that area. I do three sets of 6–8 reps, which gives me a total of nine sets for the complete routine.

There are several other deltoid movements that I've used with success over the years. For

With Machine Overhead Presses, be sure to fully straighten your arms at the completion of each repetition of this excellent movement.

Actually, I think that the overall choice of exercises is less imporant than the choice of the specific exercise for each of the deltoid heads. If you pick a movement for each head and use the Pre-Exhaustion Principle, I'm sure that you'll make some excellent deltoid gains regardless of the exercises you use.

My routine is very intense, so it's suitable only for advanced women bodybuilders, and particularly those women who are competing. If you're a beginning bodybuilder—or a woman simply interested in staying well-toned and physically fit—I'd suggest you do only one light warm-up circuit and one heavier circuit of the three deltoid exercises. Intermediate bodybuilders should do the warm-up and two additional circuits.

Regardless of your training experience, the deltoid routine I've described will work well for you if you do it three times per week and scale it to your own exercise capacity. I *know* it will work, because it helped me win the Ms. Olympia title!

example, I like Upright Rows for the side and rear delts, as well as for the deltoid-trapezius tie-ins. And when I've had access to pulleys, I've benefited greatly from Cable Side Laterals for the medial deltoids and Cable Bent Laterals for the posterior delts.

Dumbbell Side Laterals are similar to Machine Side Laterals. Keeping your arms slightly bent throughout the movement, slowly raise the dumbbells in semicircles from your sides up to shoulder height.

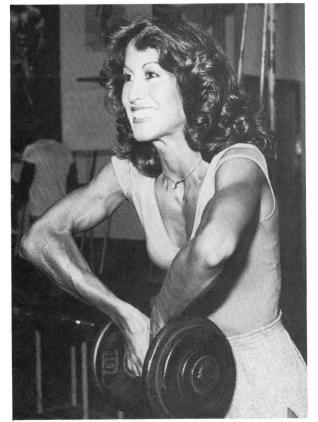

Upright Rowing can be done with either a dumbbell (as illustrated) at left and above or a barbell. Simply pull the weight from a position with your arms straight upward to chin level.

A Posterior Graduate Course

by Mandy Tanny

There is a nucleus of a shapely body. If you can see glute muscles accentuated, you know a woman is in shape.

For one thing, they are hard muscles to build. For another, they are in an area where a woman carries most of her fat.

Good glutes give a woman an animal attraction. She looks capable, ready to spring into action. The muscular appeal is basic, and men love it.

Glutes need a lot of direct work. They are in an area that gets sat on a lot. It is the first area to go on a woman's body because it is large and too often unused. They begin to succumb to the pull of gravity by the age of 21, and maybe as late as 25, but amazingly a lot of young women have not seen them at all. These women have never exercised.

Glutes are sexy. Any woman can have them with reasonable work. Unlike the bosom, there is always hope for the glutes. She is lucky if she is abundantly equipped in both these areas. She has hit the jackpot.

I get tired of people hailing a skinny pair of legs and a big bust as a great figure. A shapely, well-proportioned body with strong glutes is more the ideal. Glutes are the mark of distinction.

I used to have just large breasts and nothing else. People would always tell me how great I looked. I believed them until I started to work out with weights. I mean until I got into serious bodybuilding training. What a transformation! Now after two years I feel I have the beginnings of a quality feminine physique.

As long as pants and form-fitting clothes are in, so will the glutes be in. You had better make the most of it. Tailoring clothes around flabby glutes isn't the answer. It's better to tailor the muscle.

The truth is, most guys love fine glutes, but most women don't have them. The term itself is déjà vu to most women. It offends the feminine sensitivity of yesteryear; nonetheless, they should look trashy but classy and a little outrageous.

You can be conservative in other areas if you wish, but don't spare the glutes. It is possible to train that so-called "cellulite" right off them. You can rid them of those hammer-marks that plague women like the pox. You can make them as smooth and glossy as the paper on a centerfold. Combined with sensible diet it is the only way you can accomplish this in that problem area.

Contrary to popular belief there is nothing like full squats to get rid of that saddle-bag fat. Until recently I had been doing many of the peripheral, supplemental exercises to get my glutes up, but I wasn't satisfied. I avoided full squats because I thought it would aggravate a knee injury I got in ballet. I also figured I had to do them with a lot of weight.

But you don't. I am only using 60 pounds for 4 sets of 15 reps. The response was amazing. Every day for two months my glutes built up a little higher. All the other exercises I had been doing for the past couple of years didn't do for me what full squats alone had done.

Valerie Coe, whose husband Boyer is a 12-time World Bodybuilding Champion, does a light set of Squats.

What's more, it had accomplished the opposite of a long-standing belief that squats would make your butt big. In fact, my hip girth decreased as the glute muscle itself rose higher. I can contribute this unique response to two things. First, the high-reps, full squats burn an enormous number of calories. Second, the supplemental peak-contraction exercises I had been doing had built peaks that remained as caps on the expanding bellies of the glute muscles.

The squat has beome the basis of my glute routine. Shaping and peaking is done with pulley kickbacks, back raises, good-morning exercise, lunge squats and hacks.

I start my routine with a two-mile jog on an indoor mechanical jogger. I like running tracks if available and convenient. Fully warmed by the run, I can launch right into squats, two sets of full squats, 15 reps each. The first set of full squats is done with feet straight ahead, the second with feet angled out. The latter position helps work the inner thighs. I use the upright machine for half squats, two sets of 15 reps with 150 punds.

I do the movements slowly, both concentric and eccentric contractions. I sink slowly into the squat position and come up with the back straight and head up. In the way of variety, which I feel is necessary for all-around development, I often do the final five reps of a set somewhat fast, stopping short of full lockout at the top, sustaining tension on the thighs until the count of 15. The fast, final reps offer the momentum to carry you past the fatigue threshold.

I consider half squats to be a position with the thighs parallel—or slightly below parallel—to the floor. Also, to keep my attention on the muscle action, I squeeze the glutes together each time I reach the top of a rep. Come up, squeeze, relax, and squat again. This prevents you from merely concentrating on the thighs which is easy to do when you are squatting.

Having pre-fatigued the greater glute mass with the basic squats, I then can go on to the detail work starting with the good-morning exercise. I use a barbell across my shoulders, and with knees slightly bent, I bow forward, my back slightly below horizontal. It's a simultaneous movement. As you go down, your rear end sticks out, your knees bend slightly, and you come up the same way finishing in a fully erect position. Come up slow and keep the tension on the glutes and hamstrings. I do three sets of 15 reps, starting with a 40-pound barbell and finishing with 70 pounds.

Next, the pulley kickback with the ankle strap is started with the leg extended back, toe touching the floor. On the first set bend the upper body slightly forward as you extend the leg back and up. Do 15 reps and rest briefly. Do not alternate legs. Continue, doing three more sets of 15 reps, but now arch the upper body back with each rep and kick the leg back as high as possible as though trying to touch the head to the foot. That's a total of 60 reps. Then go on to the other leg and do the same. A 15-second rest between sets should be max. Starting with the toe pointed in, I gradually rotate the foot

Rear Leg Kicks under cable tension strongly stress the buttocks muscles, firming and shaping them.

shoulders, and takes strength and balance. I only occasionally do them, three sets of 15 reps with each leg, alternating legs. You step all the way forward to a low lunge position, back upright, and return, using the rear foot as a pivot. You can make the glutes work hard if you concentrate on them. This exercise will put grace and decisiveness in your step.

Like I said, my glutes didn't really start to peak until I did squats. The combination of mass building and peaking exercises does for the glutes what barbell curls and one-arm concentration curls do for a bodybuilder's biceps. You get the ultimate look in size and shape.

Furthermore, I have found that six sets of squats do more for my legs than a mile run. At this point I have done both of them extensively. The squats have filled in all those trace hammer marks that even running could not do. They have given my legs and glutes the shape I desire. I believe they do as much for your heart and lungs as running. Aerobically a series of squats sets seems to satisfy all the requirements for that kind of training. You huff and puff, and your pulse rate thumps along at high rate. I think you sustain that well-known training effect where energy is drawn from your body fat stores. It is

laterally several degrees on each subsequent set which ensures full coverage of the muscle with good peak contraction. This one gives the hips a high, full, rounded look. Remember, the first set should be primarily a warmup. I use about 35 pounds on the selector, but I would suggest about 20 pounds for the beginner.

The fourth exercise is the back raise done on the special piece known as the roman chair. I do this movement slowly, all the way down and all the way up and back for 30 reps, one set only. I concentrate on keeping the tension on the glutes except at the bottom where I let them relax for a second. At the top of the movement I prefer to hyperextend the back, forcing the glutes to fully contract. Also, during the course of the exercise I rotate the foot in for several reps and out for several reps, the same as in the kickbacks.

The one-leg lunge squat is closely related to the regular squat in the way of developing glute mass. This is an advanced exercise, especially when you are holding a barbell on your

Lisa Lyon does a set of Lunges to stress her hip, thigh, and buttock muscles.

an educated guess on my part, but from the results I have gotten since doing squats I am convinced that squats have actually cut down the overall size of my rear end and given it more shape where it counts. Isn't that what bodybuilding is all about?

Let me assure the women who think that squats will build that big behind they are so afraid of. The glutes are a big muscle, and big muscles don't build easily. Misconceptions run rampant. Most women today are going around with atropied glute muscles—no strength, no tone and no shape. That's because they don't use them. Ordinary activity of daily living doesn't help. Direct exercise is necessary.

Another nice advantage of well-developed glutes is that you can wear shorts, pants, dresses or rags with equal effect. Tailor the body. Never mind the clothes, they will fall into place.

My entire glute workout (which I combine with my leg workout) takes about 30 minutes. I do it twice weekly. It is really worth it. Any woman can do it. It's a sure way to become a thoroughbred.

The annual Ms. Olympia competition is the acme of women's bodybuilding, and the winner is generally acknowledged as the world's best woman bodybuilder. In the 1980 Ms. Olympia show, the finalists (left to right) were Corrine Machado-Ching (4th), Aubey Paulik (2nd), Lynn Conkwright (3rd), Rachel McLish (1st), and Stacey Bentley (5th).

Thigh Training for Strength and Tone

by Lisa Lyon (as told to Laura Mishima)

Women are finally learning what men knew all along: physical fitness through weight training and bodybuilding can improve the quality of your life. The year 1979 will go down in history as the beginning of *serious* women's bodybuilding, and I feel privileged to have been an integral part of it.

After guest posing at both the Diamond Cup and Mr. Olympia competitions, I can report that the popularity of women's bodybuilding has never been greater. My goal is to promote the sport, and thanks to Joe Weider and Arnold Schwarzenegger in particular, I have had this opportunity. The acceptance and support I have received from my male bodybuilding peers have served as a vote of confidence, but perhaps even more encouraging is the increased participation of women throughout the nation.

The women I meet are no longer interested in exercising just to lose weight. The idea of firming, toning, strengthening and conditioning the body now appeals to them. Some have visions of entering contests in the near future; others simply want to improve themselves. It's for the benefit of all of them that Joe has asked me to write this article.

Most women in America lead sedentary lives.

And we all know where the resulting extra weight lodges—the hips and thighs.

The key, of course, to trim, shapely thighs is consistent, disciplined exercise—i.e., exercise done on a regular basis. But build up the volume and intensity of training gradually. As you try my thigh routine, keep in mind that I train 3½ hours six days a week (not that you have to do that). But before I began bodybuilding two years ago, I danced ballet on and off since childhood, and had danced flamenco for eight years. In other words, I was already in pretty good shape when I began weight training.

Evaluate your current physical condition and set reasonable goals for yourself. Never push or strain to the point of inviting injury. If you're overweight, adhere to a strict but sensible diet because no amount of exercise will compensate for overeating. If you have been bodybuilding or weight training for some time, you will have fun with this routine and experience fast results.

My goal is to build my thighs—to strengthen this area and actually increase its size. I realize that most women want to reduce rather than enlarge this area, but my program will work for them, too. They should simply follow the instructions but substitute higher repetitions with less weight (or even no weight). Also, they should run a couple of miles before working out. The speed of the run will be secondary to the duration, because the goal is to burn calories.

When women talk about losing weight, they usually mean firming the thighs and getting rid of cellulite. Men don't seem to develop fat in this area; the reason is their hormonal balance.

There is good reason for the higher percentage of body fat in women. Fat which accumulates in the breast, hips and thighs is instrumental in the process of childbearing. It

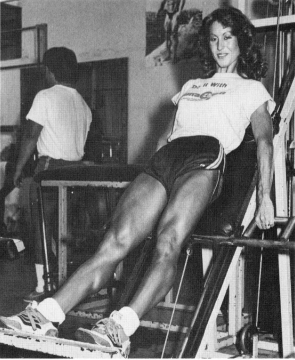

Rachel McLish demonstrates correct form in the use of Hack Machine Squats. This concentrated movement primarily develops the front thigh muscles.

acts as a cushion, protecting the baby.

When a woman's fat level is down, say, below 10% (the average is 35%), she may not have a normal monthly menstrual cycle. Without the necessary reserves, she is not equipped to sustain a pregnancy.

With this genetic factor in mind, I have learned to appreciate the natural lines of the feminine physique. No matter how hard I train, I will never develop the broad shoulders and narrow hips inherent in the male structure. Of course, each woman is unique in her body type, so you must be realistic in setting goals. I have always said, "Let reason dictate."

If you're looking for the number one exercise to firm and strengthen the legs, I'd say it's running. I run an average of two miles daily, plus I run stairs or sprints. As mentioned, a distance run is best for women who want to reduce. To build and shape the thighs, the more intense activities of sprinting or running stairs are best.

But women with a wider-than-average hip region may have trouble running. Even women with narrow hips may suffer from knee or other bone irritations. And running alone will not focus on the thigh's problem area, namely, the inner thigh. That's one area that my series of four basic exercises will hit directly.

The first exercise, the Squat, has often been called the single most effective exercise for overall body conditioning. The Squat exercises the quadriceps, leg biceps and gluteus maximus. For thighs, I recommend Hack Squats, because Full Squats tend to work the gluteus rather than focusing on the thighs. Squatting with heavy weight will build the entire body. Again, if your goal is reducing, use light weight or no weight, but do more reps.

If you're inexperienced in weight training, be sure to use a spotter and do not add weight to the bar until you have perfected your form. On the other hand, if you are squatting with more than your body weight, use a lifting belt to relieve strain on the lower back.

1. Squat *(for photos, see page 62)*

Stand with your feet hip-width apart and knees over toes. If you want to increase your range of motion, stand on a one-inch board. Make sure the knees are over the toes to avoid knee injury. Injuries are not caused by a particular exercise, but from carelessness and improper form.

Rest the weight on your trapezius, not the neck, with your head up and shoulders open (not hunched over). Slowly lower your body, keeping your back as straight as possible. A half-squat will work the thighs. If you squat through a full range of motion, you will also help firm and build your gluteus.

If you are straining and cannot control the movement properly, the weight is too heavy. Reduce the weight and practice correct form. I only use 135 pounds in the Full Squat, but have used up to 285 pounds doing the Bench Squat on a machine. A reasonable weight for someone not interested in gaining muscle tone is 65 pounds. If you want to reduce, do four or five sets of 10–12 reps with half your body weight. The motion is similar to the *plié* movement in ballet.

If you are interested primarily in burning calories and reducing, you should rush to the next exercise. I rest between sets, then proceed to the next exercise, the Leg Press, which complements the Squat by working the leg biceps and gluteus.

2. Leg Press

This exercise is done on a machine. You lie on your back with the weight above you, or sit, if the first apparatus isn't available. I prefer to use the Lying Leg Press machine because your range of motion is greater. The Seated Leg Press can become a partial extension if the seated machine is not adjusted properly. Generally, you can lift more weight on the seated machine so don't be afraid to increase poundages.

Lie on your back with your feet shoulder-width apart. Again, your feet and knees should be in line as you lower the weight until your knees touch your chest. This exercise must be done slowly and with complete control. Most women are stronger on this leg exercise than on others and are able to handle more weight, but if done improperly, the exercise will cause knee problems.

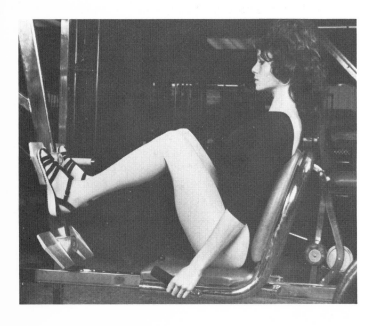

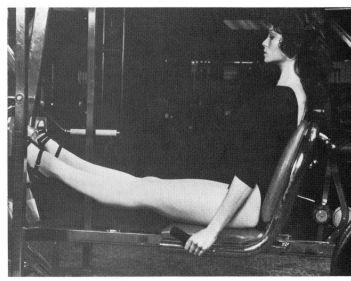

The next two exercises are to be supersetted—i.e., done in succession, then repeated for the required number of sets. They are done on the same machine.

3. Leg Extension

The Leg Extension exercise is done sitting on the machine with your feet curled under a padded bar. Use a comfortable weight. If you're trying to reduce, use 30 or 40 pounds and do as many as 20 reps per set. Lift the weight slowly under complete control—do not jerk it up or let it drop down. Never fully extend the leg to a straight position.

For variation, I turn my toes out, in and forward to experience different effects. Toeing in works the outer thigh, and toeing out exercises that hard-to-reach inner head. Keeping the toes straight forward works the entire thigh region. The important thing is to focus on the muscle you are working and help *think it* to its best form.

4. Leg Curls

Using the same machine as in the previous exercise, turn over and assume a face-down (prone) position. Again, do 15–20 reps slowly and with control. You may want to develop a rhythm, lifting the weight to a count of five and lowering

it even slower. Keep your hips and buttocks down if you want to work the thighs. Sometimes I lift my buttocks intentionally to develop the gluteus, but this is mainly a leg biceps exercise.

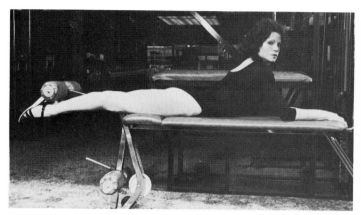

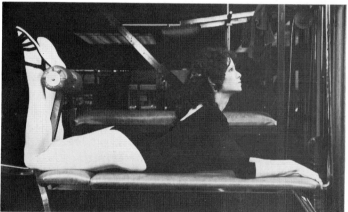

Both the Leg Extensions and Leg Curls constitute one set. Repeat this series after you have done Squats and Leg Presses.

I usually run *before* my thigh workout to warm up, because I do calf work after my thigh routine and this completely bombs my legs. A woman's legs are 23% stronger than her upper body. You'll be surprised at the maximum poundages you can achieve in your leg exercises.

Finally, if you experience cramps or muscle spasms, do not play the martyr and continue with your program. Always stop and treat the injury. The cramps are probably due to a deficient diet, incorrect form or exercising too intensely. Get to know your body and its basic needs, and it will work for you. See you at the gym!

Put Shape in Your Calves

by Lisa Elliot

Why do otherwise serious women bodybuilders neglect their calves? Why do they go into contest after contest without developing the gastrocnemius muscles, those upside down hearts at the back of their lower legs?

When fully developed, your calves can be a beautiful, sensual and powerful muscle group. Flaring upward and outward on each side from the ankles and then tapering to the knees, the calves of a good woman bodybuilder have a shape that no other body part can equal!

The calves are very important to a competing bodybuilder. They're clearly visible in any pose, regardless of the angle at which you stand. Front, side or back—it's impossible to hide poor calf development. So why not try the calf routine that expanded my "hearts" from 13½" to 15½" in only a year?

Perhaps bodybuilders tend to neglect their calves because they're so difficult to develop. Since you've been on your feet at least several hours a day most of your life, the muscle tissue in your calves has become tough and resistant to exercise. It takes hard and heavy training to induce growth.

The first—and most important—technique I would suggest that you use is the Weider Muscle

A Florida resident, the incredibly muscular Lisa Elliott has been bodybuilding for less than two years!

Priority Principle. This principle advocates training a lagging muscle group first in your routine, when your physical and mental energies are highest.

The only time I'd consider not working calves first is on a thigh-training day, because your Squats will be very shaky when you've exhausted your calves first. After a good calf workout, the muscles will quiver, which makes it tough to squat. So on leg days I'll either skip calf training altogether, or do only a light pumping calf routine at the end of my whole workout.

A second Weider technique I use extensively is the Overload Principle. To keep a muscle group growing, you have to progressively increase the resistance you use in every exercise. I've personally found that heavy weights and low reps are best for the calves, because this both overloads the muscles and keeps them constantly under tension (a la the Weider Continuous Tension Principle).

Using a full range of motion is especially important in calf workouts. Always stand with your toes and the balls of your feet on a high block so you can stretch your heels as far as possible below the level of your toes on each rep. This gives your calves a complete stretch every repetition, particularly when you keep your knees locked in Standing Calf Raises.

At the top of each rep I rise up as high as possible. This is the only way you can fully contract your calves. Moving them from a complete stretch to a complete contraction and back to a stretch on every rep will boost those twin "hearts."

I've also found it essential to keep my mind fully on my workout when I train calves, *thinking* growth into them. Like Arnold Schwarzenegger, I visualize my calves as mountains of muscle while I bomb them.

Beginners should start out easy, being sure not to overdo it. Train the calves only three times per week every other day.

If you're totally new to weight training, do only one set of Calf Stretches and one set of weightless Toe Raises. (For the correct way to perform this movement and all other exercises in my calf routine, look at the exercise descriptions and photos included with this article.) Do about 30–60 seconds of Calf Stretches and one set (20 reps) of Toe Raises off a block in the first workout.

It's essential for complete beginners to start out very easily and progress gradually in both volume and intensity. Jumping into a full workout right away will just give you very sore calves.

To avoid muscle and joint injuries, always do a warm-up set at the beginning of every workout. Do either Standing Calf Raises or Seated Calf Raises, and try for 20–30 reps, using either a light weight or none at all. Actually, the beginner's routine just presented will make a fine calf warmup as you continue to progress through the intermediate and advanced levels of bodybuilding.

From the one-set beginner's routine, add one extra set each week (e.g., do two total sets the second week, three total sets the third week, etc), until you are up to this full beginner's routine:

1. Calf Stretch: one minute.
2. Standing Toe Raise: 3 × 15 (three sets of 15 reps with a light weight in the range of 50–75 pounds).
3. Seated Toe Raise: 3 × 10 (light weight—start with 20 pounds, or whatever is comfortable for you, and work up).

On the three sets of Standing and Seated Toe Raises, switch your toe position from toes out to toes straight ahead to toes in, changing the position each set. Each of these toe positions emphasizes a different area of the calf muscle. You can build a complete calf only by regularly doing Toe Raises in each of the three toe positions.

If you feel you need added muscle mass on your shins, you can do 2–3 sets of 20 reps in a Reverse Toe Raise. Simply stand with your heels instead of your toes) on a block of wood and raise and lower your toes (instead of your heels) over a full range of motion.

Another tip: concentrate on your calves as you walk up a stairway. Try stretching your heel below your toes and then rising up on your toes. You'll find this a good supplement to your regular calf workout.

The beginning routine can be followed for six weeks by those women with competitive aspirations. And for women concerned with personal appearance and fitness, this workout can be used indefinitely.

As you gradually increase the intensity and duration of training over the six weeks, you can work up to a four-day-a-week (Mondays, Tuesdays, Thursdays, Fridays) intermediate routine such as this:

1. Calf Stretch: 1–2 minutes.

2. Seated Toe Raise: 3 × 10 (moderately heavy weight).
3. Standing Toe Raise: 3 × 8–10 (moderately heavy weight).
4. Universal Toe Press: 1–2 × 12–15 (moderate weight).

Again, it's essential to use all three toe positions on each exercise. On the Toe Press, it's okay to use only 1–2 toe positions per workout, but over the course of a week, you should end up using all three positions equally. And be sure to concentrate on your calves as you climb stairs.

Since I'm a competing bodybuilder, I find that I need to train my calves very hard 4–6 times per week to keep making gains. After you've done about four months of steady training, you can use my current workout.

1. Calf Stretch: 2–3 minutes.
2. Standing Toe Raise: 3 × 8–10 (280–320 lbs).
3. Seated Calf Raise: 3 × 8 (120–140 lbs).
4. Nautilus Toe Press: 2 × 8 (180–200 lbs).
5. Donkey Toe Raises: 2 × 6–8 (200–230 lbs).

Use all three toe positions and keep stressing those calves when walking up stairs. At the competitive level, you can even add *running* up stairs to your daily workouts. Close to a contest I do a lot of this. It's excellent for my heart—and great for my "hearts!"

CALF EXERCISES

Calf Stretch

Facing a wall, place your hands on it at about shoulder height and width, fingers toward the ceiling. With your arms and body straight, walk backward slowly until your body is leaning forward at a 45-degree angle to the floor. In this position, force your heels toward the floor, stretching your calves. If you can bring your heels all the way down to the floor, walk backward another half-step. You can also alternately stretch one calf at a time, allowing the free leg to bend weight slightly.

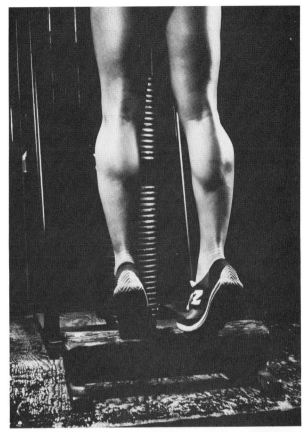

Standing Toe Raise

Load a heavy weight on a Standing Calf Machine. Place your toes on the block, bend your knees, fit your shoulders under the yokes and straighten your legs. Then simply rise up and sink down over a full range of motion.

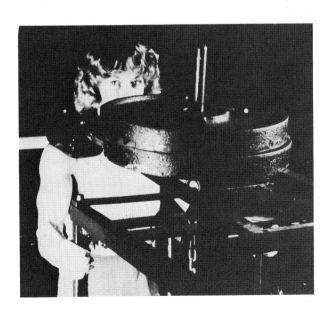

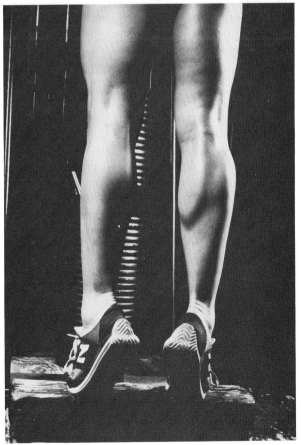

Seated Toe Raise

Load up a Seated Calf Machine and sit on the seat. Place your toes on the toe bar and wedge your knees under the knee pads. Release the stop bar by pushing it forward and then rise up and down on your toes. Seated Toe Raises are an excellent movement for the soleus muscles, which lie under your heart-shaped gastrocnemius muscles.

Universal/Nautilus Toe Press

Adjust the Universal or Nautilus Leg Press Machine's seat back as far from the pedals as possible, and place the pin where you need it in the machine's weight stack. Sit in the seat and put your toes on the bottom edge of the machine's pedals. Straighten your legs and then flex and extend your feet.

Donkey Toe Raise

Place your toes on a block and bend over so your torso is parallel with the floor. Brace yourself with your hands on the edge of a bench. With your partner sitting on your lower back astride your hips, rise up and sink down as you do in all the other calf exercises.

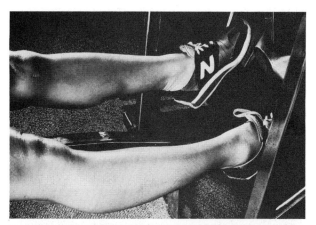

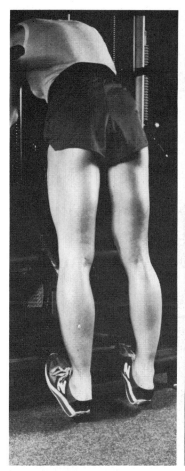

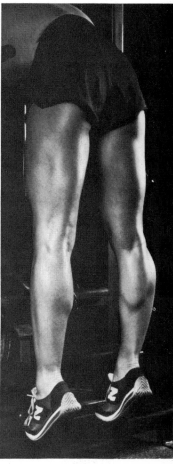

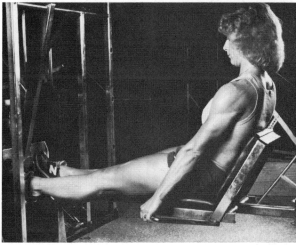

30 Instant Collaborative Classroom Banners

BY DEBORAH SCHECTER

SCHOLASTIC
PROFESSIONAL BOOKS

NEW YORK • TORONTO • LONDON • AUCKLAND • SYDNEY
MEXICO CITY • NEW DELHI • HONG KONG

For Peter,
in memory of Petey

Cover design by Norma Ortiz
Cover and interior illustrations by Rusty Fletcher
Interior design by Kathy Massaro

ISBN # 0-439-11103-X
Copyright © 1999 by Deborah Schecter
Printed in the U.S.A.

Contents

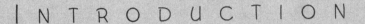

Have a Banner Year!

Welcome to *30 Instant Collaborative Classroom Banners*. In this book you will find patterns for easy-to-make banners that will help your students build their writing and reading skills—and beautify your classroom all year long. Just photocopy the write-on patterns and invite children to personalize their pages. Then tape them together for an instant, irresistible banner that's ready to display. Your students will be pleased and proud to see their individual contributions joined together in a banner that celebrates the uniqueness of every child in your class. You'll also find that the collaborative process helps foster cooperation and teamwork among your students and respect for one another's work.

Besides brightening the walls of your classroom, the banners will provide an ongoing invitation to reading. Most of the banners contain rhyming text that will help your students build confidence as readers and take pleasure from the experience of reading. Students will enjoy reading their own contributions as well as those of their classmates. In addition, the banners can be used as teaching tools to support learning in other curriculum areas such as math, social studies, and science. (See Banners Across the Curriculum, page 6.)

From All About Me (September), to We Had a Great Year! (June), the banners in this book are organized by month to help you and your class celebrate favorite themes, special occasions, holidays, and seasonal changes throughout the school year. But please feel free to pick and choose from the topics and make any of the banners whenever you wish.

I hope that you and your students will enjoy using the patterns in this book to have a banner year!

—*Deborah Schecter*

How to Use This Book

Step-by-Step to Beautiful Banners

1 Make enough photocopies of each pattern so that each child has one page. (Note: Some banners, such as We're in _____ ! (pages 18–19), ABC Circus Train (pages 23–25), and We've Got the Reading Bug! (pages 31–32), have more than one pattern page. Let children take turns coloring the first page of these banners. A few banners, such as Dig Those Dinosaurs! (pages 50–52) and Thank You, Community Helpers (pages 55–57), have several patterns from which children can choose.

2 Discuss the topic and read the prompt on the pattern page with your class.

3 Let children use developmental spelling to write their responses on scrap paper or on self-sticking notes. Let children who are not yet writing dictate their responses to you. Help children edit their work and copy the edited version onto the pattern page.

4 Invite children to illustrate their patterns with crayons, markers, or colored pencils. If the pattern page contains a shape or door to cut out (indicated by dotted lines), have children do this now. Then encourage them to use craft materials to decorate and embellish their creations. (You'll find specific how-to's and suggestions, listed by topic, on pages 8–17.)

5 Let children help put the banner together by taping their pattern page to the others. Help them line up those that continue from page to page.

6 Display the banner on a bulletin board, on a wall, from the ceiling, or in the hallway. Many of the banners also look great as pennants. Clip side by side on a clothesline strung across your classroom in an area that's away from traffic. Banners that have patterns in different shapes, such as the Welcome Winter! mitten (page 37) and the Happy New Year! balloon (page 40), work especially well when displayed this way. You don't even have to tape together the pages. Any way you choose to display them, the banners will be a delightful invitation for children to read, share, and enjoy.

Banners Big and Small

☀ You might choose to do some of the banners as a whole-class activity and make long banners that include the work of each child in your class. Or let children take turns working in groups of five or six to make mini-banners.

☀ Many of the shape banners will work horizontally, vertically, or diagonally.

☀ Some of the banners have flap doors for children to open. Hang these banners low enough so that children are able to reach and read them.

Banners Across the Curriculum

Language Arts Use the prompts on the banners as springboards to other writing experiences. Invite children to elaborate on their responses by writing stories, poems, letters, reports, and so on.

Math Students' patterns can easily function as bar graph banners. For example, when doing Colors Galore!, Pet Parade!, or It's Groundhog Day!, arrange students' pattern pages in rows or columns according to their responses. Help children interpret the data by asking questions such as "What color is the favorite of most children in our class?" "What color is the least favorite?" "How do you know?" "How many children say that blue is their favorite color?" "Do more children in our class prefer blue or orange?" and so on.

Our Favorite Colors

Orange	
Blue	
Pink	
Yellow	

Social Studies Celebrate the diversity of your students by using banners such as All About Me and Friends Are Stars! as springboards for discussion about the ways people are alike and different. Hooray for the Holidays! can be used to help children learn about the history and traditions of the different winter holidays children in your class celebrate. Ask family members to visit your class to share and explain their holiday traditions.

After making Thank You, Community Helpers, consider inviting to your class people that children named and hold a party in their honor. Then find out about the possibility of hanging the banner in a prominent place in your community, such as the local library or post office, for everyone to enjoy.

Science Celebrate seasonal changes with Time for Fall, Welcome Winter!, and It's Spring! Encourage children to look outside and observe the changes that occur during each season and to incorporate these into their writing and illustrations. Use What's the Weather? to help children track changes in the weather from day to day. The Happy Earth Day! banner can be used to link social studies and science and help children become aware of ways they can help protect the earth.

Art Talk with students about ways to make their banners stand out. For example, writing with markers or crayons will make them more visible and easier to read at a distance than pencil. Students may also want to use crayons to shade the background of their pattern pages for a finished product that's colorful and bold. Suggestions for adding other embellishments such as ribbons, string, and natural objects are included in Month-by-Month Teaching Tips, pages 8–17.

Turn Banners Into Books

When it's time to take down a banner to make room for another, consider turning it into a collaborative class book to place in your classroom library for children to read and enjoy. Children will also be proud to share their banner books with family members. (Place the books in large, self-closing plastic bags, enclose a letter that describes the banners and their learning benefits, and let children take turns bringing them home.)

* To make a class book, first carefully peel off the tape that joined the banner pages together (or unclip from clothespins). Then make a front and back cover out of heavy construction paper or oaktag. Photocopy a blank pattern page masking out all of the text except for the title. Invite a child to color and then paste it to the front cover. For the shape banners, use the pattern to trace and cut out front and back covers in the same shape.

* Use blank paper to create a title page, a dedication page (complete with copyright information and the name of your "publishing house"), a page for family members to share their comments, and an About the Authors and Illustrators page.

* Stack together the covers and inside pages and punch holes in the top or left-hand side of the book. Put the book pages in order and bind together with O-rings, paper fasteners, ribbon, or yarn.

To make an accordion book, remove the banner from the wall, leaving the pages taped together. Fold the pages back and forth so that they lay one on top of another. Make a front and back cover by cutting two pieces of oaktag slightly larger than the book pages. Use a glue stick to attach each to the back of the first and last pages. Ask a volunteer to decorate a blank pattern page and glue it to the front cover. Then use a piece of ribbon to tie the book closed.

Month-by-Month Teaching Tips

SEPTEMBER

We're in _____! (pages 18–19)

Make this banner at the start of the school year to help the children in your class get to know one another and to develop a sense of community. Use the pattern showing the front of the school bus (page 18) to fill in your students' grade and your name. Invite a child to draw a picture of you driving the bus! Then give each child a copy of the pattern on page 19. Let children draw a picture of themselves in the window, complete the prompt, and sign their name. To assemble the banner, begin with the front of the bus and tape to the other pattern pages.

All About Me (page 20)

After completing the prompt, invite children to personalize the body outline to resemble themselves. Have yarn, ribbon, fabric scraps, wiggle eyes, glue, and other arts and crafts materials on hand for them to enhance their work. Then have children cut out their shapes and tape together so that the figures look like they are holding hands.

Birthdays Are Great! (pages 21–22)

Have each child complete the pattern on page 21. For a special effect, let them decorate their cake with "icing" (use glitter glue that comes in tubes). Then make multiple copies of the candle patterns on page 22. Have children cut out and color the correct number of candles for the birthday they will be celebrating this year. Have them tape these to the top of their cake pattern.

To display this banner, you might have children sequence the pages by birthday month and date. Have children decide on a start date (birthdays that fall at the beginning of the school year or at the start of the new year in January). Or, instead of a whole-class banner, hang a mini-banner each month made up of children's birthdays for that month. Create a special banner for children whose birthdays fall during the summer months.

ABC Circus Train (pages 23–25)

Put the engine and the caboose patterns (pages 23 and 25) at either end of this banner. Assign each student a letter of the alphabet to fill in on his or her pattern page. (Use the caboose for the letter *Z*.) Invite students to draw things that have names beginning with the letter as well. Then use colorful round stickers to link the cars in the train.

Your class may also enjoy making an ABC Animal Circus train. Help students research the names of animals for each letter of the alphabet. Have books with pictures of different animals on hand to help children with their drawings. The alphabet book series by Jerry Pallota (Charlesbridge Publishing) is an excellent source for ideas. Books in this series include *The Icky Bug Alphabet Book, The Bird Alphabet Book,* and *The Furry Animals Alphabet Book.*

OCTOBER

What's the Weather? (pages 26–27)

Use this banner to help children track daily changes in the weather. On a daily basis, let children take turns filling in a pattern page and pasting on the appropriate weather symbol from page 27. Or, if children prefer, they can draw a picture that shows what the day's weather is like. You can make separate banners to record the weather for a week or a month. After several weeks or months, review the banners with students and talk about any weather patterns that emerge.

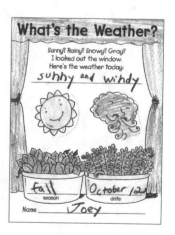

Time for Fall (page 28)

If you live in an area where leaves change color in the fall, invite children to glue colorful leaves around the edges of the banner. Or let children create their own autumn leaves cutting them out from construction paper and painting or coloring them in fall hues.

Happy Halloween! (pages 29–30)

Begin this banner with the spooky house on page 29. Then hand out copies of page 30 and invite children to draw a picture of themselves dressed up in what they'll be wearing on Halloween. Encourage children to enhance their pictures with yarn, glitter, wispy pieces of cotton (spiderwebs), and other craft materials. When the banner is up, children will have fun trying to guess one another's costumes. For extra-spooky fun, darken the room and shine a flashlight on each child's contribution as classmates make their guesses.

You might also want to use students' creations to make a Costume Banner Graph. Survey the types of costumes children drew, then come up with four or five categories to put them in, such as Animals, TV and Movie Characters, Scary Characters, and so on. Make a label for each on a sheet of construction paper and let children take turns placing their costume in the appropriate column on the graph. Then ask them to study the graph as you ask questions such as "How many children are going to be dressed as animals?" "What kinds of costumes are most common?" and so on.

NOTE

Before making this banner, you may want to send a letter home to parents to be certain the celebration of Halloween doesn't conflict with the religious beliefs of children's families.

NOVEMBER

We've Got the Reading Bug!
(pages 31–32)

Use this buggy banner to let children share their favorite books during National Children's Book Week—celebrated during the third week of November. Begin this banner with the bug face on page 31, writing in your name under the bug's smile. Have children respond to the prompt on page 32 and draw a picture from their favorite book in the book shape provided. To decorate the bug's body, children can add three-dimensional antennae crafted from pipe cleaners and glue on glitter and sequins.

Friends Are Stars! (page 33)

This banner will help foster the spirit of friendship and create a caring and supportive atmosphere in your classroom. Here's a fun way for the "stars" in your class to share this banner. Have children use glow-in-the-dark crayons to write their responses to the prompt and color the stars on their pattern page. Clip the completed patterns to a clothesline, or tape together and display on a bulletin board. Then create a cozy atmosphere for sharing. Dim the lights and invite children to take turns shining a flashlight on their contribution to the banner as they read it aloud.

We Give Thanks (page 34)

Make and display this banner before Thanksgiving. Then, before children go home for the holiday, give them their completed page along with extra blank copies for family members. Suggest that children invite each of their family members to complete a pattern. The patterns can then be used as festive and meaningful place mats for their holiday celebration. (Suggest that children glue the completed patterns to sheets of construction paper.)

DECEMBER

Hooray for the Holidays!
(pages 35–36)

Use page 35 to provide a cheery start to this holiday banner. Have each child complete a copy of page 36. Then let them use glue and white, silver, and gold glitter to add a snowy sparkle. Or have students glue their pages to a sheet of dark blue or black construction paper and then use a paintbrush and white paint to dab on a snowflake border. For teaching ideas to use with this banner, see Banners Across the Curriculum, page 6.

Welcome Winter! (page 37)

These mittens will look warm and cheery clipped to clothespins and hung on a clothesline strung across your classroom. You can also use them to play a sorting game with your class. Invite children to use crayons or markers to make their mittens bright and colorful, adding additional patterns and designs if they like. Then have children sit in a circle on the floor with their mittens in front of them. Ask: "How might you sort the mittens into two groups?" List children's ideas. Then pick an attribute such as color (keep it a secret!), and instruct children, one by one, to clip their mittens to either end of a clothesline, forming two groups (for example, blue/not blue). When half the mittens have been hung, challenge children to guess where the remaining mittens belong on the line. Afterward, ask children to guess the attribute you used. Repeat the activity, inviting students to take turns choosing new criteria for sorting. (Activity adapted from "Why Do Mittens Work?" by Lynne Kepler, *Instructor* Magazine, January/February 1996.)

Our Favorite Foods (pages 38–39)

Give each child a copy of each of the pattern pages. Let children cut out a favorite food from page 39 and paste it inside the lunch box or draw their own picture of a food they especially enjoy.

Use this banner as a springboard to a discussion about good nutrition. Discuss children's favorite food choices. What other foods would children need to add to their lunch boxes to make a healthy lunch? Help students investigate the food pyramid and the kinds of foods that make up a well-balanced diet.

JANUARY

Happy New Year! (page 40)

The balloons on this banner will look great clipped to a clothesline strung across your classroom. For fun, let children tape to the bottom of their balloon a piece of colorful string or ribbon.

After making this banner, help children research when and how different cultural groups celebrate the New Year. For example, the Jewish year usually takes place in early autumn, following the Jewish calendar, and the Chinese New Year falls on the first day of the new moon, usually between January 21 and February 20.

Snowman Show! (pages 41–42)

Give children a copy of both pattern pages. Invite them to dress up their snowman using the clothing patterns provided. Or let children bring in natural items such as small sticks for arms and pebbles for eyes. You might also have on hand craft materials such as pipe cleaners, fabric scraps, yarn, crayons, markers, construction paper, pom-poms, buttons, and wiggle eyes.

For a math tie-in, challenge children to decorate their snowmen using only geometric shapes such as circles, squares, triangles, rectangles, and so on. When the banner is up, invite everyone to discuss the different ways the shapes were used.

100 Days of School— Hooray! (pages 43–44)

Start this banner on the first day of school. Assign each child a number between 1 and 100. Then give children a copy of the pattern page to complete on their assigned day. Use the pattern on page 43 to start your parade of elephants, then match up the elephant's tail with the trunk of the elephant next in line, adding a new elephant each day. Children will have fun seeing this banner grow and wrap around your classroom! If your room's not big enough, perhaps you can use a long hallway and invite the rest of the school to join in your count-up. (For extra fun, ahead of time, challenge children to bring in objects representing their number— for example, 12 shells, 35 peanuts, 72 pennies, and so on. Put the items in plastic bags and tape to each child's elephant.)

You can also use this banner as a basis for daily math problems. Ask your class questions such as "How many days are there before we reach the 100th day of school?" "Can you point to a number on our banner that is greater than 11?" "Less than 42?" "What number comes between 71 and 73?" "What number is 2 more (or 1 less) than 10?" and so on.

FEBRUARY

It's Groundhog Day! (page 45)

Make a Groundhog Day prediction bar graph with this banner. Arrange students' pattern pages in rows or columns according to

their predictions. Ask questions such as "How many children in our class think the groundhog [will/will not] see its shadow?" and "Do most children think the groundhog will see its shadow or not?" Then wait for the big day to see whose predictions are correct!

Valentine Guess-Who! (page 46)

Before making this banner, assign each child a secret valentine. Children then write a clue about themselves on the front of the heart and label it with the name of their valentine. To make the secret flap door, give each child a rectangle of light-colored construction paper slightly larger than the door. Have children cut out the flap door along the dotted lines and fold it back along the solid line. Then show them how to glue the construction paper onto the back of the heart so it covers the cutout opening, trimming any excess. Have children draw a picture of themselves and write their name on the construction paper, then close the door. Let children decorate their hearts with bits of paper doilies, ribbons, sequins, and other craft materials. On Valentine's Day, children will have fun trying to guess each other's secret valentine!

We've Lost Teeth! (page 47)

This is a great banner to do during Dental Health Month in February, but you may prefer to make it near the start of school to track children's tooth loss during the year. Let children personalize the face and then color in a tooth for each one they lose.

MARCH

It's Spring! (page 48)

Here's another banner that will look great hanging from a clothesline. Let children tape to the bottom of their kites strings and kite tails made out of construction paper, tissue paper, or fabric scraps. When the banner is up, the kites will look as if they're about to sail up, up, and away!

Happy St. Patrick's Day! (page 49)

To get children to respond to the prompt on this banner, ask them to think of something green that they would like for St. Patrick's Day (green pizza, a green dog, and so on). Then invite them to investigate different shades of green. Have them start with the different greens found in large boxes of crayons. Next, challenge them to find examples of the color green from different sources (pictures in old magazines, paint color cards from paint stores, used gift wrap, wallpaper sample books, clothing catalogs, fabric scraps, and so on). Have students group the samples by varying shades, cut them into shamrock shapes, and add a multitone green border around the edges of the banner.

Dig Those Dinosaurs! (pages 50–52)

Children's responses to the prompt on this banner offer a great graphing opportunity. Let children choose a dinosaur from the three patterns provided—Stegosaurus, Triceratops, and Apatosaurus. After completing their patterns, children can then arrange them on the wall in rows or columns according to their responses. Then ask questions such as "What different colors do children in our class think dinosaurs were?" "How many children think dinosaurs were [fill in color]?" "Do more children in our class think dinosaurs were [fill in color] or [fill in color]?" "What color do most children in the class think dinosaurs were?" and so on.

APRIL

April Fools! (page 53)

Celebrate April Fools' Day and the beginning of National Laugh Week by inviting children to share their favorite jokes and riddles on this banner. To make the patch-pocket flap door, follow the directions for Valentine Guess-Who! on page 14. Children write the answers to their riddles on the construction paper under the flap door. Then invite them to add yarn hair, colorful makeup, and other decorations to their clown.

Happy Earth Day! (page 54)

Make three-dimensional earths for your Earth Day celebration. Have children respond to the prompt and then cut out the earth pattern along the dotted lines. Then have each child trace the pattern onto a sheet of construction paper and cut it out. Instruct children to put a thin line of glue around the edge of the construction paper shape, leaving the top edge without glue. Then have them glue together the two shapes. When the glue is dry, show children how to gently stuff the earth with facial or bathroom tissue and glue the opening closed. Use clothespins to clip the earths to a clothesline strung across your classroom.

Thank You, Community Helpers (pages 55–57)

Begin this banner with the pattern on page 55. Let children choose one of the building patterns from pages 56 and 57 and write "Pet Store," "Post Office," and so on, on the sign above the door. To make the flap doors, follow the instructions for Valentine Guess-Who! on page 14. Children draw a picture of the person they are thanking under the flap. For ways to use this banner, see Banners Across the Curriculum, page 6.

MAY

Pet Parade! (pages 58–59)

Use this banner to kick off Be Kind to Animals Week in the first week of May. Everyone in your class can contribute to this banner, even if they don't have a pet. Have children complete the prompt on page 59 and draw a picture of their perfect pet. Have craft materials on hand for decorating (craft feathers for birds, shiny sequins for fish scales, cotton or fake fur for furry creatures, and so on). Ask a volunteer to decorate page 58, and use it start off your banner in a festive way.

You can also use students' pages to make a graph. Arrange them on a wall in rows or columns according to students' responses. Ask questions such as "Would more children in our class like to have a dog or a cat?" "Which pet do most children wish they had?" "Which pet do the fewest children wish they had?"

Colors Galore! (page 60)

After filling in their favorite color on the peacock's body, ask children to draw on each feather pictures of things that are associated with that color. When the banner is up, play a game of I Spy. Invite children to take turns giving clues about an object on one of the peacock feathers. For example, a child might say, "I spy something on our banner that is yellow. It is a long fruit." (banana)

Family Photos (pages 61–62)

Invite children to choose one of the frame patterns then fill in the number of members in their family. Explain that a "family" may include anyone who lives with them, including pets! Then invite children to paste a photo or draw a picture of their family inside the frame. This is a great banner to display on open house nights or other occasions when children's family members visit.

JUNE

We Took a Class Trip! (page 63)

Make several of these banners to celebrate the field trips your class takes during the year. Display them in a hallway outside your classroom to let students share their field trip experiences with other classes. Afterward, compile children's pages into a class photo album and place in your reading center for children to read and reminisce about the different trips they've taken. (See page 7.)

We Had a Great Year! (page 64)

This banner is sure to generate warm remembrances of the year your class has spent together and lively discussions of good times that have been shared. You might want to save this banner to display at the start of the next school year. Your new class will be curious to learn about the things that your previous students enjoyed and that they can look forward to in the year ahead! To make the flap doors, follow the directions for Valentine Guess-Who! on page 14.

M _____

We're in

!

In the summer I liked to _____,

that was *my* favorite thing to do.

Now I can't wait to _____.

How about you?

Name _____

All About Me

Some kids tell funny jokes.
Others are great in art.
What makes me special?
What sets me apart?

_____

_____

Name _____

Birthdays Are Great!

Birthdays are grand, birthdays are great.

Here is the day that I celebrate:

I will be _____ years old!

Name _____

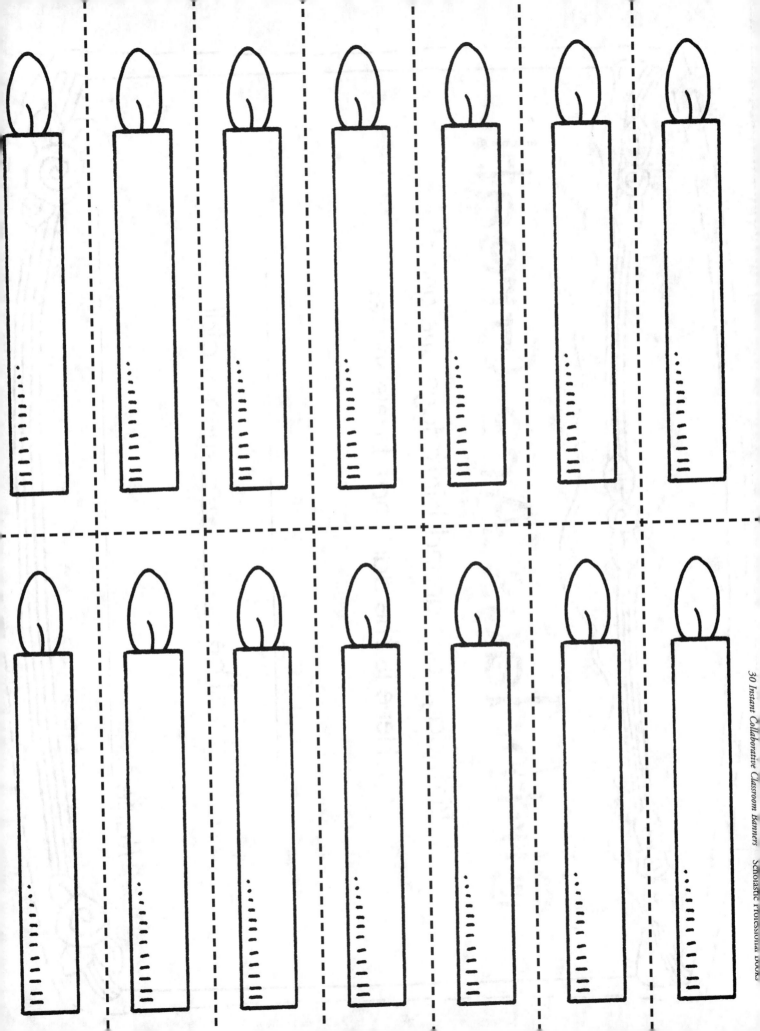

ABC
Circus Train

The letter_____ is dandy.

When I want to spell _____,

it comes in very handy!

Name _____

30 Instant Collaborative Classroom Banners Scholastic Professional Books

The letter _____ is dandy.

When I want to spell _____,

it comes in very handy!

Name _____

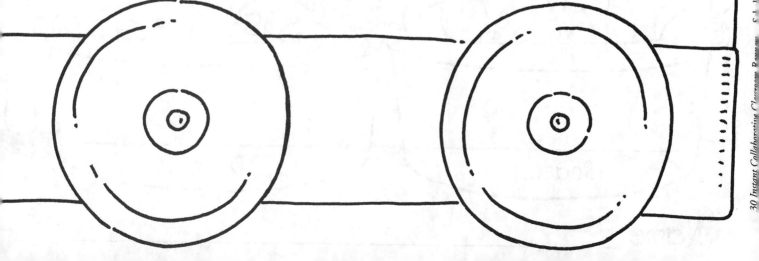

What's the Weather?

Sunny? Rainy? Snowy? Gray?
I looked out the window.
Here's the weather today:

_____

_____ Season

_____ Date

Name _____

Time for Fall

Crunchy leaves—red, yellow, and brown!

It looks like fall has come to town!

My favorite thing about fall is

_____

_____.

Name _____

Happy Halloween!

It's Halloween,
let's give a spooky cheer!

KEEP OUT!

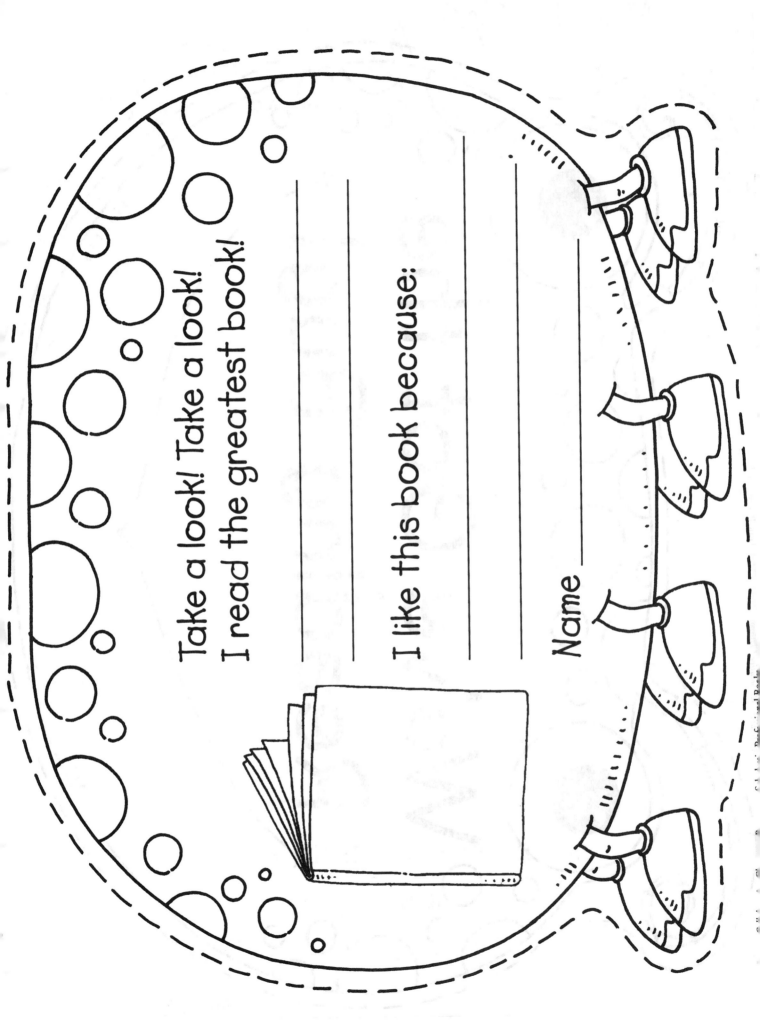

Take a look! Take a look!
I read the greatest book!

I like this book because:

Name

Friends Are Stars!

A friend is fun. A friend is true.
A friend is someone who

_____

_____

_____

Name _____

We Give Thanks

For family and friends,
pie and turkey, too.
Thanksgiving's the time
we say thank you!

I am thankful for

_____

Name _____

Hooray for the Holidays!

Hip, Hip, Hooray!
Let's give a cheer.
The winter holidays
are here!

30 Instant Collaborative Classroom Banners   Scholastic Professional Books

My family celebrates

_____

[name of holiday]

Here is something special
that we do on this holiday:

_____

_____

Name _____

Welcome Winter!

Slide on the ice?

Jump in the snow?

In winter I like to _____.

I thought you'd like to know!

Name _____

Our Favorite Foods

Munch, munch, munch.

_____

are my favorite foods for lunch!

Name _____

Draw another favorite food in the space above.
Then cut it out and add it to your lunch box.

Happy New Year!

I want to sing so all can hear
my special wish for the brand new year!

_____

_____

_____

Name _____

Snowman Show!

I made a snowman,
then dressed it up with care.
Now it has a funny face
and fancy clothes to wear!

Name _____

100 Days of School— Hooray!

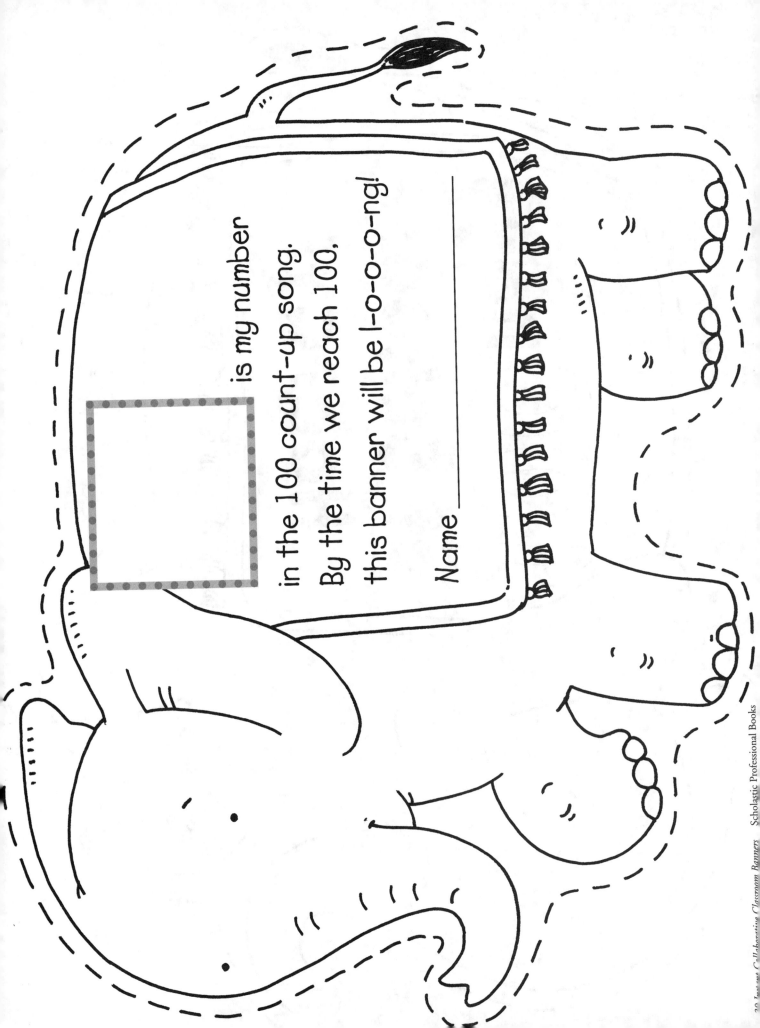

_____ is my number
in the 100 count-up song.
By the time we reach 100,
this banner will be l-o-o-o-ng!

Name _____

It's Groundhog Day!

Will winter stay, or will it go?

Will the groundhog see its shadow, yes or no?

I predict: _____

Name _____

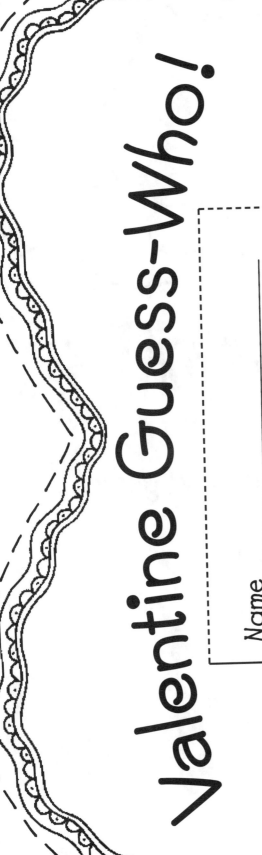

Valentine Guess-Who!

Name _____

Who's your secret valentine?
Read this clue: _____

_____

_____

Now open this door . . .
Guess who!

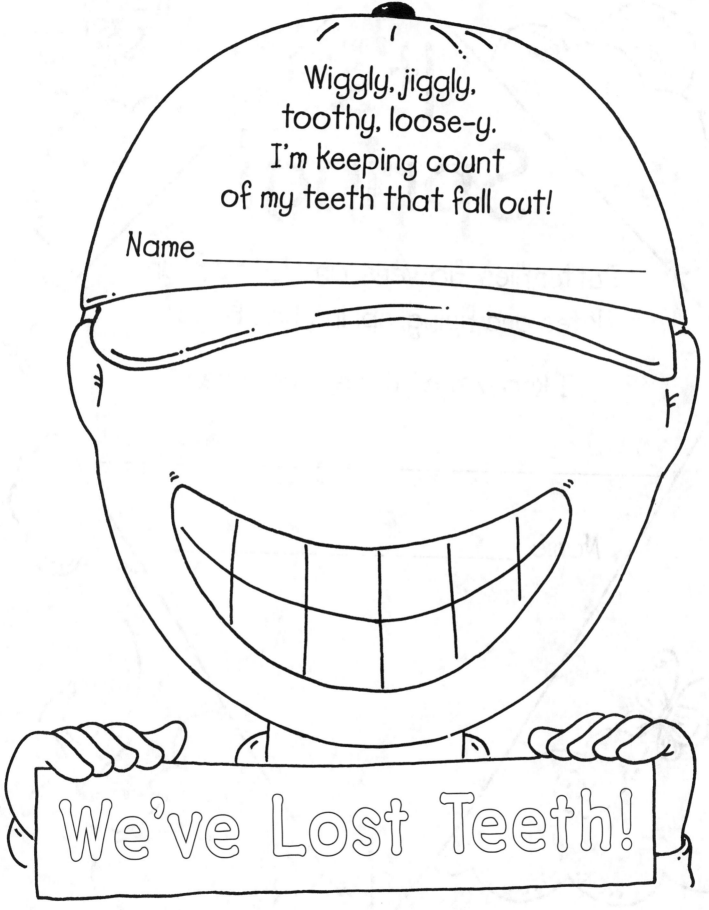

Wiggly, jiggly,
toothy, loose-y.
I'm keeping count
of my teeth that fall out!

Name _____

We've Lost Teeth!

It's Spring!

Butterflies, flowers, and lots of fun,
kites are flying, spring has begun!

I know that it's spring when

_____

Name _____

Happy St. Patrick's Day!

Leprechauns and shamrocks—
everything's green!
On this day of the Irish,
that's how it seems!
I would like a green

_____.

Name _____

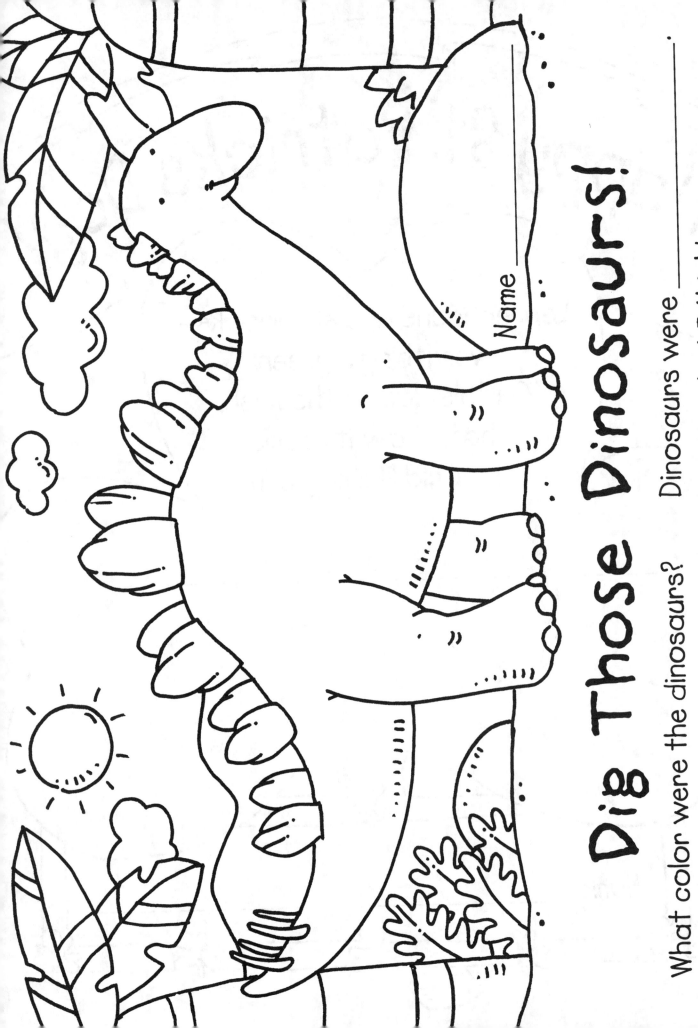

Dig Those Dinosaurs!

Name _____

What color were the dinosaurs?

Dinosaurs were _____

Red, green, or bright pink?

That's what I think!

30 Instant Collaborative Classroom Banners · Scholastic Professional Books

Dig Those Dinosaurs!

What color were the dinosaurs?

Red, green, or bright pink?

Dinosaurs were _____

That's what I think!

Name _____

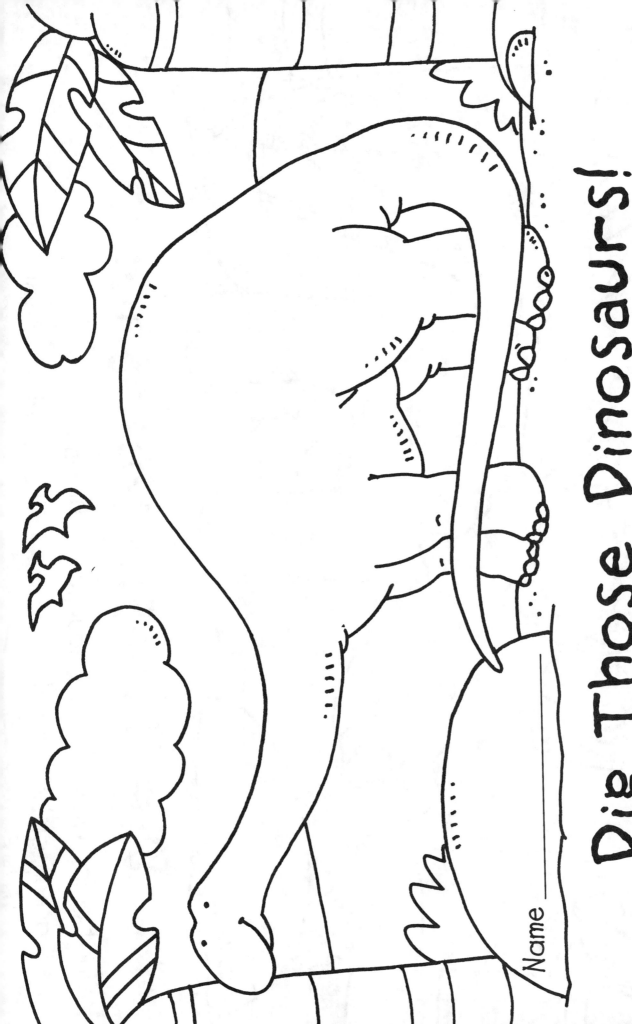

Dig Those Dinosaurs!

Name _____

What color were the dinosaurs?

Red, green, or bright pink?

Dinosaurs were _____

That's what I think!

April Fools!

Giggles and laughs
and riddles all around.
It's April Fools' Day.
Let's all be clowns!

Read my riddle!

_____
_____
_____
_____

Open this door for the answer!

Name _____

Happy Earth Day!

Happy animals
and colorful flowers,
taking care of the earth
is in our power!

I help take care of the earth by

_____

Name _____

30 Instant Collaborative Classroom Banners   Scholastic Professional Books

Lots of people help us
each and every day.
Thank you to . . .

_____

That's what I want
to say!

Open the door to meet this person.

Name _____

Lots of people help us
each and every day.
Thank you to . . .

_____

That's what I want
to say!

Open the door to meet this person.

Name _____

Colors Galore!

Red, yellow, green, blue,

My favorite color is _____

Yes, it's true!

These are things that come

in my favorite color:

Name _____

Family Photos

Some families are big. Others are small.

In my family, there are _____ of us in all.

Name _____

Family Photos

Some families are big. Others are small.

In my family, there are _____ of us in all.

Name _____

We Took a Class Trip!

Our class went to _____.

What part of the trip did I like the best?

Here's a picture. See if you can guess!

Name _____

We Had a Great Year!

What was *my* favorite thing about school this year?

Open the doors and *my* answer will appear!

Name _____

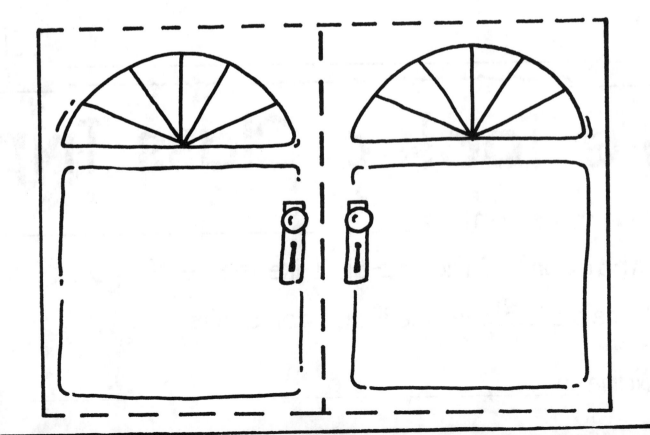